Making Space for Millennials

....

A Blueprint for
Your Culture, Ministry,
Leadership and Facilities

Barna Group

Knowledge to navigate a
changing world

A Barna Report produced in partnership with
Cornerstone Knowledge Network

CONTENTS

INTRODUCTION: DESIGNING WITH MILLENNIALS IN MIND

The eldest Millennials—born between 1984 and 2002—turned 30 in 2014. As a generation, they have been called everything from the "next greatest" to a tribe of narcissists—but whatever else we might call them, "kids" won't fit for much longer.

Millennials are coming into their own as grownups. Sure, they are putting their own spin on adulthood, just as they've remixed cultural expectations about family and friends, institutions and information, consumption and creativity. But they cannot (and should not) be ignored or written off because they relate to the world under a different set of assumptions than their generational predecessors. The church needs Millennials to continue Christ's mission of redemption, restoration and reconciliation in the world. And Millennials need communion with Christ and his Body to bring wholeness and meaning to their fractured, frenzied lives.

Many faith communities and Christian organizations are struggling with how to make space for Millennials—not just appealing space in their buildings and gathering places, but also space in their institutional culture, ministry models and leadership approach. This groundbreaking Barna Report, produced in partnership with Cornerstone Knowledge Network (CKN), is an indispensable tool for designing with Millennials in mind. You'll get to know Millennials as a generation and discover what impact their shared values, allegiances and assumptions will have on your church or organization as you make space for their ideas and influence. You'll read Millennials' perspectives on worship and community spaces, and hear from practitioners in each of the four design arenas—culture, ministry, leadership and facilities—about how the next generation of Christian adults is shaping their approach to form and function.

This report is drawn from two main sources: Barna Group's ongoing work to shed light on the Millennial generation and major new research commissioned by the Cornerstone Knowledge Network. CKN came to Barna Group with one guiding question: *How can we create transformational space for and with Millennials?* We designed the resulting study to assess both abstract ideas, such as perceptions about Christianity and the American church, and preferences regarding tangible built environments. We wanted to take a fresh look at the practical realities of working with the emerging generation, focusing mainly on young Christians but not excluding Millennials from other faith traditions.

The Barna team has conducted more than 30,000 interviews with Millennials over the past decade; that body of work has been leveraged in the creation of this report. Adding to that foundation, the CKN study surveyed a nationally representative sample of Millennials from across the faith spectrum. (If you're into research details, you can find cross-tabulated data tables and read about the study's methodology in the appendices.)

One of the unique aspects of this landmark study was our use of visual survey questions. In addition to conventional word-based questions, the online survey also included questions with image choices as the answers. This type of visual polling provides useful insights into today's design-oriented and image-drenched, Instagram and Pinterest generation. Browsing through this report, you can get an immediate sense of the kinds of images Millennials respond to on a broad range of topics, including work, home, faith, Christianity and church.

It became obvious, as early research progressed, that a quantitative survey alone would not be enough to paint a three-dimensional picture of how Millennials interact with Christian organizations in various spaces. We needed in-depth interviews to complement the national survey, with participants giving feedback in real time, on location. And so we took two groups of Millennials, one in Chicago and one in Atlanta, on a field trip to church facilities in their area. Here you'll find their responses to the places they encountered, as well as practical questions based on their insights to help you make meaningful decisions in your faith community.

Making Space for Millennials is a handbook for turning information *about* Millennials into connections *with* Millennials in your church, school or organization. Whether you are a pastor, an educator, a youth or young adult ministry leader, or a nonprofit or business leader, this resource is designed to help you make the most of your current and future partnerships with Millennials.

FIVE POINTS OF CONNECTION

Before we dig into the meat of this report, we'll give away the most significant conclusion: There are five major reasons Millennials stay connected to a Christian community:

1. *Cultural discernment*—engaging with the wider culture, as a faith community, to assess and respond biblically to its effects on human flourishing

2. *Life-shaping relationships*—consistent, long-term friendship with at least one older Christian adult who invests time and resources into their lives

3. *A firsthand experience of Jesus*—the confidence, through seasons of doubt and pain, that comes from having personally experienced God's revelation in Christ

4. *Reverse mentoring*—being valued for the knowledge, skills and energy they can offer to older members of the community of faith

5. *Vocational discipleship*—whole-life spiritual formation that includes understanding their work as a God-given calling

There is no simple, one-size-fits-all blueprint for an institutional culture, ministry program, leadership structure or building that is guaranteed to reach Millennials. But these five points of connection are the outcomes we must seek as we make decisions for our churches and faith-based organizations. Are our structures serving to achieve these ends? If not, we're probably not yet making enough space for the next generation of disciples.

Let's look first at the gap between Millennials' cultural assumptions and the cultural values held by many churches and faith-based organizations ... and how engaging in cultural discernment together can bridge the divide.

"Culture" can mean many things. And since it's a word that gets tossed around a lot, particularly in conversations about generational differences, we should all agree here at the beginning on a definition. Is it art, or an appreciation of the arts? (As in, "Patrons of the Boise Philharmonic are so cultured.") Is it the customs, institutions and achievements of an ethnic group or nation? Or maybe the cultivation of bacteria or tissue in a petri dish?

Of course, the word "culture" refers to all of these. But when we talk about "digital culture" or "church culture," for example, we are talking about outward expressions of the inward attitudes of a particular social group. In this definition, culture is a reflection of worldview: the values, assumptions and allegiances shared among a group.[1] When we define culture this way, it's easier to keep in mind the many differences between smaller groups—regional, ethnic, religious, political and, yes, generational.

Your church has a culture: one influenced by the broader culture around it and specific to your region, local community and member demographics. If your faith community is in North America and your members are mostly North American, your church or faith-centered organization shares many worldview assumptions with your region and country. For instance, most people in your church would likely agree that freedom is good, education is important and children should be protected from harm. These are worldview assumptions shared by most North Americans. They are so much a part of us that we don't have to think about them; in fact, we *don't* think about them, which is why we call them assumptions! They seem self-evidently true, not even worth mentioning.

In a similar (but smaller) way, every church has a distinct culture. The inward worldview shared within a community of faith is expressed outwardly in leaders' decisions, in choices about where to invest resources, in the design of ministries, facilities and leadership structures. Most of the time,

Culture is a reflection of worldview: the values, assumptions and allegiances shared among a group.

to most people in the church, the assumptions that drive these choices aren't noticeable. They don't think about them because they share the worldview within which these assumptions make perfect sense.

But then a person or group of people comes along who doesn't share that worldview, for whom those assumptions are not self-evidently true.

Millennials—those born between 1984 and 2002—are part of our broader North American culture, but they also share within their generational cohort a unique set of values, assumptions and allegiances. In *You Lost Me: Why Young Christians Are Leaving Church . . . and Rethinking Faith*, David Kinnaman, president of Barna Group, suggests that watershed cultural shifts taking place as Millennials emerge into adulthood are significantly changing their worldview from the perspectives shared by older generations. These changes can be broadly categorized in terms of *access*, *alienation* and *authority*.

Never before has a generation emerged into adulthood with nearly limitless *access* to diverse people, ideas, products and information at the click of a mouse or swipe of a finger. The oldest Millennials got their first e-mail accounts and cell phones in junior high. They've been texting for 10 years or more. Not since high school have they had to "look it up in the dictionary" or "find it in an encyclopedia"—and the youngest Millennials have never done so. You may have used digital tools as long as or even longer than the young adults connected to your community of faith. But if you are a Gen-Xer, a Boomer or an Elder, you didn't *become you* with the world at your fingertips. Instant, almost unlimited access—which Millennials have had since they began their journey into adulthood—has shaped how they learn, the ways they relate to and interact with the world, and their expectations for church and Christianity.

In addition to having constant and nearly unrestricted access, Millennials are coming of age at a time when many of the institutions and structures that undergird North American society have faltered. Broken promises, fallen leaders and exposed corruption have led Millennials to feel *alienated* from once-foundational institutions. The educational and economic systems that promised and delivered the American Dream to earlier generations have not come through for Millennials, who are twice as likely as older workers to be unemployed. Likewise, the institution of family has undergone a seismic upheaval over the past 30 years. From the financial crisis, to the BP oil spill, to sexual abuse scandals in churches, Millennials have seen corruption at all levels of leadership in almost every type of institution.

Which brings us to *authority* . . . or a lack thereof. Between myriad voices competing for Millennials' attention and their skepticism about institutions, many are not sure who can be trusted. Pastors? Celebrities? Professors? Scientists? Bible teachers? Politicians? Sports legends? That guy on YouTube with a hundred thousand followers who proves, going verse-by-verse through the Book of Revelation, that Christ will return on July 14, 2017? Earlier generations slapped "The Bible Says It. I Believe It. That Settles It!" stickers

In a modular world, everything can be taken apart and reassembled in a new pattern.

on their bumpers. But Millennials have heard evidence suggesting that early biblical manuscripts are unreliable, that power-hungry church leaders suppressed hundreds of other "gospels." *Maybe the Bible doesn't say it after all. And even if it does, how do I know it's true?* Access and alienation have led many Millennials also to question authority.

Access, alienation and authority are potent forces with enormous culture-shaping power. And the values, allegiances and assumptions—the worldview—these forces are creating in the next generation may not fit well within the existing culture of your church.

Let's look at a few of the ways Millennials may find it hard to fit in at church, and what your faith community can do to make space for their cultural expressions.

MODULARITY

Jimmy Stewart once gave an interview in which he described working in the movie industry during the era of the "studio system." He would go to the studio every weekday, he said, and do whatever they told him. If they were shooting a picture and he was in it, he would film that day. If they didn't have a shoot scheduled, he practiced his singing, dancing or elocution, or made public appearances or gave interviews—whatever the studio had planned. At the end of each day, he went home.

Actors—and everyone else in the movie business, for that matter—have a very different experience today. Instead of being under long-term contract to a studio, they jump in and out of projects, each with a contract of its own. Instead of commuting to a 9-to-5 job, they go where the work is, often living on location for months at a time and shooting at all hours of the day and night. If they want professional training or media exposure, they arrange it themselves or hire a manager to make it happen.

The top-down, highly organized studio system has given way to a freelance system in which actors and film crewmembers are responsible to cobble together a career for themselves out of numerous independent relationships and opportunities.

As you can imagine, this means greater freedom for modern Jimmy Stewart-types such as Tom Hanks or Meryl Streep—but it also means greater risks for small-timers. The vast majority of actors are not movie stars. They are bartenders and receptionists and retail clerks who cobble together a living even as they try to cobble together a career.

This cultural expression is *modularity*, and it is the new way our lives—from work to education to relationships—are organized. In a modular world, everything can be taken apart and reassembled in a new pattern; pieces of life are combined as desired or as necessary. Pieces that no longer fit are moved or even discarded. Once upon a time, in the not-too-distant past, "family" and "work" and "church" were more monolithic. Like working under contract in the Hollywood studio system, a commitment to one or more of these aspects

PASTORS, YOUTH WORKERS & MENTORS

• How does your faith community's culture reflect your shared worldview—and how might it conflict with the values, allegiances and assumptions of the Millennials in your community?

• How well is your faith community adapting to the new cultural reality of modularity—and what can you do less of, more of or differently to minister effectively to and with the next generation?

• What are you doing to train teens and young adults in cultural discernment—and how well are you dealing, as a community, with different cultural expressions of "what to think" and "what to do"?

of life was a soup-to-nuts deal. It was all or nothing. But increasing modularity means these monoliths are being subdivided into ever smaller pieces.

What does this mean for the community of faith?

First, it means people's needs are changing.

Consider family. According to North American worldview assumptions that have been in place for generations, a family is two married people of opposite sexes and their biological children. But in recent decades, variations on that cultural expression have become more common than the original theme. Cohabiting couples with and without children; single parents; same-sex partners with and without children; adoptive families; stepfamilies; surrogate parents; single friends away from home who band together in a tribe—each of these household types is becoming more common as families piece themselves together based on personal tragedies, goals and preferences. And each of these situations involves real people with real social, emotional and spiritual needs. Are God's people in a place to meet these needs? Or are we waiting and hoping for the day when the pieces of "family" are reassembled in a way that aligns with our worldview?

Or consider the different needs created by the changing career landscape. Fewer and fewer people in your community have steady, 9-to-5, Monday-to-Friday jobs. The economy will likely continue to recover, but as it does the pieces of "work" are getting smaller for everyone, not just people in the movie business. Increasingly, each person is expected to piece together his or her own career with short-to-midterm assignments rather than long-term permanent employment. As a result, they have different needs than in times past: sustainable work-life balance in a market that is constantly shifting; safe, affordable and dependable childcare outside "normal" business hours; the ability to juggle financial obligations and uncertain streams of income; a place away from home (and the kids) to work for a few hours or to network for the next opportunity. The pressures created by these needs have social, emotional and spiritual impact. Are God's people in a place to help? Or are we waiting and hoping to meet monolithic "spiritual" needs that are unconnected to the everyday practicalities of life in a modular world?

Second, if modularity is changing what people need *from* churches, it is also changing how people *engage with* churches. As in the realms of family and work, people are piecing together "church" according to their preferences and experiences.

Think about the cultural expressions of "church" offered by the local community of faith: inspiring Bible teaching, Christian fellowship, a place to serve, a time of worship. In our modular world, we can get great Bible teaching from a John Piper or Beth Moore podcast, fellowship on Facebook or Skype, an opportunity to serve at the crisis pregnancy center and worship on the I Heart Radio app. We could even "attend" the local megachurch in our pajamas by streaming the Sunday worship service on our Web browser.

WHEN A TEXT MESSAGE COMES IN, I USUALLY STOP WHAT I'M DOING TO CHECK IT.

42%

36%

49%

35%

I THINK MY PERSONAL ELECTRONICS SOMETIMES SEPARATE ME FROM OTHER PEOPLE.

I GET FRUSTRATED WHEN I HAVE CONFLICTING PIECES OF INFORMATION.

67%

60%

40%

34%

I GET ANXIOUS WHEN MY PHONE DIES WHILE I'M OUT.

I CHECK MY PHONE ....

56% 49%

...FIRST THING IN THE MORNING

54% 39%

...RIGHT BEFORE BED

12% 6%

...IN THE MIDDLE OF THE NIGHT

Like work and family—and, increasingly, everything else—church is no longer a package deal. And this is especially true for Millennials, for whom modularity is not an unfamiliar, unfortunate side effect of globalization and hyperconnectivity, but just the way things are. The challenge for faith communities is to help young adults identify what pieces of "church" are inadequate, misshapen or missing in their modular lives and then help them rebuild or fill in the gaps—and connect the pieces of family, work, church and faith into a cohesive, whole, Jesus-shaped life.

The calling is not to compete with the other pieces but to make space to help Millennials make sense of them all.

HOME, FAMILY & WORK

As faith communities make room for Millennials to do this work of whole-life discipleship, it may be helpful to get a glimpse of their preferred cultural expressions of various pieces of life. As part of the Barna/CKN survey of a nationally representative pool of Millennials, we showed participants four images and asked them to choose the one that best corresponds to a phrase such as "feels like home," "feels like family" and "a place I would like to work."

· · · · · · · · · · · · ➤

When we asked which of the four images most "feels like home," two out of three respondents chose the forest scene (64%)—far more than all the other images combined. The next-most-popular image was a beach scene, but only about one in six felt it was evocative of home (16%). Even fewer selected the cityscape (12%), and fewer than one in 10 picked the picture of a road trip (8%).

It is no surprise that the nature-themed images in this series are the top selections. As we will explore at length in chapter 4, "Facilities," nature is a big deal for Millennials. This may be due in part to the fact that they're the first American generation to grow up with high awareness of human impact on the environment. In addition, since they are more urbanized than any other generation, theirs may be a case of absence making the heart grow fonder. And while the overall trend is people moving further into rather than away from the "urban jungle," many cities are undergoing a nature-centered revitalization. For example, Boston created a greenway on the old stretch of I-93 that now runs underground. New York has done something similar with old elevated railways. These changes to existing urban landscapes are in part a response to Millennials' fondness for green spaces and being out of doors.

Another aspect of the most popular "home" image is its suggestion of restfulness and human connection. There is a comfortable-looking picnic table in a shady, cozy spot that holds out the promise of relaxing conversation,

The church has a role to play as a welcoming, stabilizing community for those who are struggling to find their place to belong.

Male	16%	Male	13%	Male	62%	Male	9%
Female	16%	Female	11%	Female	64%	Female	7%
Married	9%	Married	9%	Married	75%	Married	7%
Unmarried	18%	Unmarried	13%	Unmarried	62%	Unmarried	8%
Single, never married	17%	Single, never married	12%	Single, never married	62%	Single, never married	9%
Children	13%	Children	10%	Children	72%	Children	6%
No children	19%	No children	13%	No children	59%	No children	9%
HS or less	18%	HS or less	10%	HS or less	65%	HS or less	7%
Some college	15%	Some college	11%	Some college	66%	Some college	8%
College Grad	15%	College grad	17%	College grad	61%	College grad	7%
<$40k	13%	<$40k	10%	<$40k	70%	<$40k	7%
$40k - $60k	7%	$40k - $60k	20%	$40k - $60k	69%	$40k - $60k	4%
$60k+	22%	$60k+	10%	$60k+	58%	$60k+	10%
Churched	18%	Churched	8%	Churched	68%	Churched	7%
Marginally churched	5%	Marginally churched	7%	Marginally churched	79%	Marginally churched	8%
Unchurched	16%	Unchurched	15%	Unchurched	61%	Unchurched	8%
Other faith	28%	Other faith	17%	Other faith	47%	Other faith	9%
No faith	12%	No faith	20%	No faith	58%	No faith	10%
White	17%	White	7%	White	69%	White	7%
Black	8%	Black	20%	Black	67%	Black	3%
Hispanic	20%	Hispanic	17%	Hispanic	52%	Hispanic	11%
Nonwhite	16%	Nonwhite	18%	Nonwhite	58%	Nonwhite	9%
Northeast	16%	Northeast	10%	Northeast	65%	Northeast	10%
South	9%	South	15%	South	70%	South	7%
Midwest	18%	Midwest	8%	Midwest	68%	Midwest	5%
West	21%	West	16%	West	54%	West	10%

Barna/CKN, October 2013, N=843 U.S. adults ages 18 to 29 years old. The segmentation percentages above are among Millennials who participated in the study.

maybe even over a meal. The cityscape and road trip images suggest less leisure and more activity, while the beach scene is more solitary.

Many Millennials have an idyllic concept of "home," but the reality is that they are far from it. First, many are *geographically* far from home. Although a good number are bunking, for the time being, with Mom and Dad for financial or other practical reasons, there are many who are moving across the country for college or to start new careers and new lives.

Jamie Tworkowski is the founder of To Write Love on Her Arms, a non-profit movement dedicated to presenting hope and finding help for people struggling with depression, addiction, self-injury and suicide. TWLOHA began in 2006 as Jamie's attempt to help a friend and tell a story. Today, TWLOHA is a source of hope, encouragement and resources for young people around the world.

What role does pop culture—from movies to music to festivals to art to surfing—play in To Write Love On Her Arms?
We talk a lot about meeting people where they are. That basically means relating to people, using language they understand, talking about things that interest them. The "pop" in "pop culture" means *popular*, which means a lot of people are already interested, or participating, in a certain thing happening in culture. If there's a story or event within pop culture that relates to pain and hope, we think that's powerful. It's a way to invite someone to think differently about something they're already thinking about.

An example of this: One of the most-read blog posts in our history was written in response to the death of Phillip Seymour Hoffman. Everyone was talking and thinking about the actor's life and death. We looked at those things through the lens of TWLOHA, and it meant a lot to see the blog connect with people. More than anything, our aim is always to be honest about the pain and struggle of life, and from that place, to point people to hope and help.

Why is pop culture so important and such a good fit for TWLOHA's message and mission?
For starters, so much of pop culture means the arts. And there's an instant depth with art because it's about feelings. Music and films have the unique ability to remind us we're alive, that it's okay to feel things and it's okay to ask questions. We think that's a great starting point for the conversation we're trying to invite people into.

Beyond that, most nonprofits require a "third thing." It's one person or organization asking another person to care about a problem impacting a third, specific group of people, often in another specific place. For us, it's more about the one-on-one. We believe every person we encounter can relate to the issues we speak to, whether it's in their own life or in the life of someone who they care about.

So wherever we go, whether it's a music festival or simply someone reading our words online, we are speaking directly to the person, not so much asking them to care about this other third thing happening in this other place, but instead simply inviting them to be honest about their own life, their own questions, their own story.

Why do you believe movies and music, particularly, are such important catalysts for healing messages?
So much of our daily lives are about performance. We go to school and we go to work and those things are mostly about "getting the job done." We aren't sure if there's a place for our humanity, for our questions, struggles, fears and dreams. So we start to buy the lie that those things should just be kept quiet. But movies and music invite us to feel again. They remind us we're human. They give us permission to consider the stories we're living and the healing we hope for in our stories and in the stories around us.

One of the ways TWLOHA really connects with people is through social media. What is the best advice you can give to people (or organizations or communities) for using social media to connect with people?
When it comes to social media, there's plenty of nonsense and noise, plenty of

people selling things and promoting things. Here are a few of our rules: Be authentic. Be conversational. Don't tweet things you wouldn't actually say. Be compelling. Be poetic. No matter how big the audience gets, remember that it's made up of individuals. It's made up of real people. Do your best to meet them where they are. Post things that move those people, encourage those people, invite and challenge those people.

When you think of larger organizations or brands that connect with people— beyond the "faceless" or "profit-driven" label—what are some brands that do it well? What makes them successful in humanizing their organization or brand?
I think charity:water is incredible. They're the ones I think of most often. From design to storytelling to finances, it seems like they can do no wrong. As for their storytelling, I love that they focus on the positive, on the solution. It's not sad images of people without water—I think that's the stuff of organizations that came before us. Charity:water invites people to be part of the solution, so you see the smiles on the faces of people the moment when a well is drilled and clean water arrives.

We also love Invisible Children. We share a lot of common ground with them in terms of when we got started and both being born from a story that we stumbled upon. They've done a great job of telling stories and coming up with creative ways people can get involved in ending the world's longest running war.

Beyond those two, everybody loves Apple. They make beautiful products that are incredibly easy to use. And they've done a great job of communicating the message that their products exist to serve the lives of people.

In what ways do you and your team work to make sure the internal structure at TWLOHA and the atmosphere of your work environment reflects your external message?
That's a hard piece to the puzzle. It's always easier to say something than to live it out. I do believe we're good at creating space for people to feel cared for. Sometimes that means helping someone from our team go to counseling—giving the time and money to make that happen. Or maybe it's giving someone time off to deal with something going on at home or with their family. We never want to be the sort of place that says, "You leave that stuff at home. You deal with that after work." We have to do our best to care for each of the people on our team, to see them as a person and not simply an employee.

As for me personally, I got comfortable standing on a stage telling people it was okay to go to counseling, and okay to take anti-depressants. But up until a few years ago, I had never taken those steps in my own life. I remember a moment when I was booked to speak at a couple events. I was going through a breakup and having a hard time. It came time to fly to do the events, and our team basically said, "You stay home. Someone else will cover those. You need to take care of you." It was humbling, but I remember feeling incredibly cared for.

EDUCATORS
& SCHOOL
ADMINISTRATORS

• How well does
your institution's
cultural expression
of learning fit with
Millennials' worldview
assumptions—and
how might you need
to adapt to educate
them more effectively?

• How do you see
modularity affecting
the learning process—
and what can you
do to help Millennials
connect knowledge
acquisition with the
other elements of their
fragmented lives?

• In what ways is
cultural discernment
a meaningful aspect
of your educational
rubric—and how
can you pass on
wisdom in addition to
knowledge?

Second, many are *socially* far from home. Their childhood friends are moving away or getting married or trying on different identities and social tribes.

They are also far from home *culturally*. They are actively redefining many of the cultural and social institutions their parents and grandparents took for granted.

And, of course, many are far from home *spiritually*, questioning the received tenets and behavioral norms of their faith in a process that is necessary if they are ever to own, for themselves, the label "Christian." (Secondary research suggests that those who experience a season of intense questioning and get serious about finding answers are most likely to have deep, lifelong faith.)

The church has a role to play as a welcoming, stabilizing community for those who are struggling to find their place to belong. Take another look at the picture in Figure 1.2 so many of them prefer. What is the emotional draw of the scene Millennials would like to come home to? How can your community of faith help them connect that longing to the other pieces of their lives?

Tolstoy famously wrote, "Happy families are all alike; every unhappy family is unhappy in its own way." Many Millennials have come from families unhappy in their own unique ways, and this may be a driving factor in their extensive remodel of "family." Most of them deeply value family, even as they broaden the concept to include a variety of unconventional forms. With all the upheaval, it is fascinating that the image chosen by a plurality to represent "feels like family" is the most traditional: a parent and child holding hands. Two out of five Millennials (42%) chose this image. (Also note the backdrop of the picture: soft grass dappled by sunlight. Nature again!)

But the difference between the top-rated image and the others is not as wide as in the preferences for home. One in four Millennials selected the group of friends at a coffee shop as their image of family (25%), and about one in five chose the picture of friends at the beach (22%). Taken together, those who preferred an image of friends exceed the number who chose the most popular, more traditional image. So while a traditional view of family still makes a strong showing, the cultural expression of friends as de facto family is as popular as the '90s sitcom.

As with "home," the church has a role to play when it comes to Millennials and family. First, the church must be a family of faith, "dear brothers and sisters" in Christ, as the apostle Paul wrote dozens of times in the Epistles. In God's family, teens and young adults are our younger siblings and deserve a place at the family table—and not the little kids' table, either! Too often we treat young people as troublesome children, rather than as heirs with us of God's glory (see Rom. 8:17).

	25%		22%		42%		11%
Male	28%	Male	23%	Male	37%	Male	13%
Female	22%	Female	21%	Female	47%	Female	10%
Married	15%	Married	12%	Married	68%	Married	6%
Unmarried	28%	Unmarried	24%	Unmarried	35%	Unmarried	13%
Single, never married	31%	Single, never married	24%	Single, never married	34%	Single, never married	11%
Children	16%	Children	20%	Children	53%	Children	10%
No children	32%	No children	23%	No children	34%	No children	12%
HS or less	18%	HS or less	23%	HS or less	45%	HS or less	13%
Some college	31%	Some college	21%	Some college	39%	Some college	9%
College Grad	27%	College grad	19%	College grad	41%	College grad	12%
<$40k	21%	<$40k	19%	<$40k	47%	<$40k	14%
$40k - $60k	25%	$40k - $60k	21%	$40k - $60k	41%	$40k - $60k	13%
$60k+	28%	$60k+	24%	$60k+	39%	$60k+	9%
Churched	23%	Churched	20%	Churched	47%	Churched	11%
Marginally churched	33%	Marginally churched	14%	Marginally churched	43%	Marginally churched	10%
Unchurched	25%	Unchurched	22%	Unchurched	41%	Unchurched	12%
Other faith	26%	Other faith	18%	Other faith	47%	Other faith	8%
No faith	33%	No faith	19%	No faith	32%	No faith	15%
White	30%	White	20%	White	41%	White	10%
Black	19%	Black	23%	Black	40%	Black	19%
Hispanic	15%	Hispanic	25%	Hispanic	50%	Hispanic	10%
Nonwhite	19%	Nonwhite	24%	Nonwhite	45%	Nonwhite	12%
Northeast	20%	Northeast	29%	Northeast	38%	Northeast	14%
South	26%	South	26%	South	39%	South	9%
Midwest	27%	Midwest	13%	Midwest	49%	Midwest	10%
West	26%	West	23%	West	38%	West	13%

Barna/CKN, October 2013, N=843 U.S. adults ages 18 to 29 years old. The segmentation percentages above are among Millennials who participated in the study.

But it's not enough to be a spiritual family. Churches and Christian organizations can inspire Millennials with a vision of a healthy, loving family of their own. They are getting decidedly mixed messages from the changing culture about the value of these roles and relationships. The Christian community can cast a vision for becoming a wife or husband, mother or father, and help young adults connect that vision to their fragmented lives.

But a compelling vision isn't quite enough, either. The faith community must

▶ Q&A WITH JIM HENDERSON

Jim Henderson is the founder of Jim Henderson Presents and Off the Map, and author of Evangelism Without Additives, Jim and Casper Go to Church, The Outsider Interviews *and* The Resignation of Eve. *Jim holds a Doctorate in Transformational Leadership and has been featured in* The Wall Street Journal, USA Today, *Fox Television and* This American Life. *Jim's mission is to "Take Jesus public." He doesn't understand why followers of Jesus have absented themselves from the broader public conversation that shapes spirituality and that is currently dominated by well-known entertainer-spiritual salespeople such as Oprah, Chopra, Palin and Beck.*

What are three things you observe about Millennials and church?

First, they're not radicals. When I became a Christian in 1968, it was all the rage to be a revolutionary, and a lot of our language reflected that. We repurposed the cultural language of the day—the activist, hippy, anti-Vietnam ethos. We adopted revolutionary language for our Jesus mission: getting more people saved and into heaven. Our apocalyptic language revealed our sense of urgency, which mirrored a cultural language and moment.

Millennials are, for the most part, not a radical bunch. That's something people my age need to understand. They aren't as black and white as we were or still are. And that's not a bad thing. I don't think what we did was sustainable. I think the best of what Millennials are trying to do is sustainable. They blur the lines between public and private piety—which might seem radical at first glance but really is just a reasonable effort to live out a whole-life faith.

Second, Millennials are disrupting the idea of full-time ministry. We have a whole subculture of professional Christians: seminaries, titles, tax write-offs. When older people grew up in church, this is how they understood what it means to be in ministry. And there was also this idea that full-time vocational ministry was a holier

profession. Millennials, in my experience, are not migrating toward those older models. Hardly any of them bring up wanting to be on staff at a big church. Instead, they have this crazy idea that you can have a "secular" profession and be in ministry. Journalists, photographers, software developers, entrepreneurs—nothing is keeping them from ministry right where they are.

They wouldn't say, "Someday I'll be in ministry." They assume they're already doing ministry. Not only that, they assume they will be accepted and valued and held in esteem by Millennials who *are* in professional ministry. The line is much more blurred between professional ministry and practicing ministry. It's a much more biblical pattern.

Third, they aren't afraid of working with non-Christians to make the world a better place. They're not conflicted theologically. Many wouldn't be comfortable calling themselves exclusivists.

They're concerned about "Jesus is the only way" language. They don't have the same sense of urgency I had as a young man to get people "saved." Matthew 28:19 and John 3:16 were my generation's "high Scripture." For Millennials, it's Matthew 25:40, "When you did it to one of the least of these my brothers and sisters, you were doing it to me!" Millennials hold a high view of the Kingdom, where humanity matters.

also take seriously our role as "family coaches," training Millennials to become wives and husbands, mothers and fathers, *of character*. Many of them have had inadequate or just plain bad models for these roles, and the family of faith can help. It's more than mentoring young couples, though that's an important part of the training; it's mentoring young women and men *before* they are couples so they have the character and relational skills to love and serve their future spouses and, eventually, children.

How do you see issues of feminism and women in church leadership impacting Millennials?

It's sad that you have to ask an old white guy so other old white guys will listen.

Since the 1970s, the feminist impulse has gotten less militant, less activist. The assumptions behind feminism—that women are valuable human beings capable of extraordinary things—are broadly accepted by our culture. Millennial women assume they have rights and intelligence. They grew up knowing that they are valuable and have important things to contribute to their communities.

White men still run the church. But Millennial women have been tested in the marketplace and they know for a fact they are just as smart, capable and gifted as men. And most of them won't accept institutional limitations. They won't resign themselves to the situation. They'll just drop out. If Millennial women aren't given opportunities to lead, create and innovate in church, they'll go elsewhere to do it. They won't stand still. All that creativity, all that giftedness, all those leadership smarts—lost to the church because of institutional stubbornness.

If you compare the church to Hollywood, you'll find we are very similar when it comes to how we treat women. The statistics are alarmingly similar. Hollywood uses women but won't let women run things. Sound familiar? We have no moral high ground. We can't even say we are better than the world in terms of how we treat women.

At the very least, we should do what Jesus did. The gospels make clear that he valued women; he trusted them with important Kingdom tasks. They were his favorite group of outsiders, and he scandalized the (male) religious leaders by treating women like insiders. We could use a little more scandal of that kind in the Christian community.

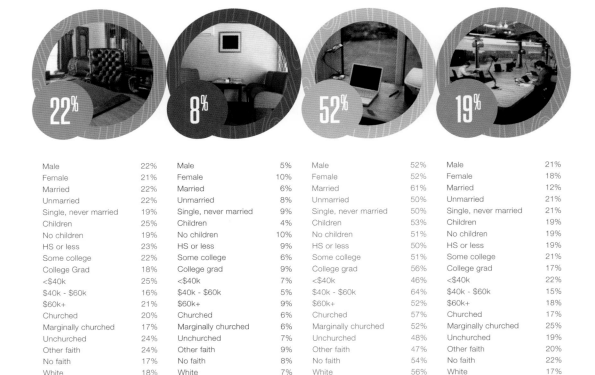

Male	22%	Male	5%	Male	52%	Male	21%
Female	21%	Female	10%	Female	52%	Female	18%
Married	22%	Married	6%	Married	61%	Married	12%
Unmarried	22%	Unmarried	8%	Unmarried	50%	Unmarried	21%
Single, never married	19%	Single, never married	9%	Single, never married	50%	Single, never married	21%
Children	25%	Children	4%	Children	53%	Children	19%
No children	19%	No children	10%	No children	51%	No children	19%
HS or less	23%	HS or less	9%	HS or less	50%	HS or less	19%
Some college	22%	Some college	6%	Some college	51%	Some college	21%
College Grad	18%	College grad	9%	College grad	56%	College grad	17%
<$40k	25%	<$40k	7%	<$40k	46%	<$40k	22%
$40k - $60k	16%	$40k - $60k	5%	$40k - $60k	64%	$40k - $60k	15%
$60k+	21%	$60k+	9%	$60k+	52%	$60k+	18%
Churched	20%	Churched	6%	Churched	57%	Churched	17%
Marginally churched	17%	Marginally churched	6%	Marginally churched	52%	Marginally churched	25%
Unchurched	24%	Unchurched	7%	Unchurched	48%	Unchurched	19%
Other faith	24%	Other faith	9%	Other faith	47%	Other faith	20%
No faith	17%	No faith	8%	No faith	54%	No faith	22%
White	18%	White	7%	White	56%	White	17%
Black	30%	Black	10%	Black	35%	Black	25%
Hispanic	19%	Hispanic	8%	Hispanic	51%	Hispanic	22%
Nonwhite	24%	Nonwhite	8%	Nonwhite	47%	Nonwhite	22%
Northeast	25%	Northeast	7%	Northeast	53%	Northeast	16%
South	24%	South	5%	South	54%	South	17%
Midwest	22%	Midwest	10%	Midwest	54%	Midwest	13%
West	16%	West	7%	West	46%	West	31%

Barna/CKN, October 2013, N=843 U.S. adults ages 18 to 29 years old. The segmentation percentages above are among Millennials who participated in the study.

When asked to select an image that reflects a place they would like to work, more than half of Millennials we surveyed (52%) chose the home office. No other image was close. The traditional executive-style office appealed to about one in five (22%); a smaller percentage chose the modern collaborative office space (16%). The coffee shop/restaurant was least appealing (8%), which is surprising given how often Millennials gravitate toward this "third place." But perhaps when it comes to work instead of social interaction, there's no place like home.

What are some ways faith communities and organizations can assess their values, allegiances and assumptions?

Among social scientists, identifying a people group's worldview involves a process called *ethnography*, a fancy word for the study of people. To assess your faith community or organization's values, allegiances and assumptions (your shared worldview), you can adapt some of the elements of ethnography to fit your context.

Ethnography begins with observing and listening to people to identify the outward cultural expressions of their inner worldview. This is called *participant observation*. You're not an onlooker; you're a participant in your community. But you're a participant who makes a deliberate, sustained effort to see and hear what is going on. Ask yourself, "What are people doing and saying?" Don't trust your memory; write it down. Be specific. Writing down specific actions and words can help us see past our own assumptions, which tempt us to interpret others' actions and words before we truly see and hear them.

Identify patterns that emerge. For instance, you might notice that people in your group tend to use "I" and "me" language, not "us" and "we," and they greet each other with bows rather than handshakes or hugs. Take another pass at observing and listening to confirm or modify your observations. Does additional seeing and hearing over the course of days, weeks or even months validate what you saw and heard the first time?

If so, ask yourself, "What do people mean by these actions and words?" The challenge here is identifying what *they* mean by their actions or words, not what *you* would mean if you did or said the same. (Assumptions again!) To uncover what a group of people mean by their words and actions, you can use another tool in the ethnography kit: *interviewing*. Pick a handful of influencers in the community and interview them, separately or in a group. Highlight for them the actions and words you have observed and ask them to discuss the values, assumptions and allegiances that lie behind these cultural expressions. Using the examples above, you and your group of influencers might conclude that your community assumes independence, rather than interdependence, and values honor above affection.

Once you have identified some of your community's values, allegiances and assumptions, try the same kind of deliberate study in an environment where Millennials hang out. What do they do and say? What do they mean by their actions and words?

Eventually you'll have the beginnings of two ethnographies that point to where the two worldviews differ. These differences are the cultural sticking points that can lead to generational hubris, unintended offenses and ministries that miss the mark.

They're also the points where grace rushes in as we do the hard, humble work of reconciliation. As Paul wrote to the church in Corinth, "We have stopped evaluating others from a human point of view. At one time we thought of Christ merely from a human point of view. How differently we know him now! This means that anyone who belongs to Christ has become a new person. The old life is gone; a new life has begun! And all of this is a gift from God, who brought us back to himself through Christ. And God has given us this task of reconciling people to him" (2 Corinthians 5:16-18, NLT).

MaryAnn Hawkins is Associate Dean and Professor of Intercultural Studies at Anderson University School of Theology. She is an ordained minister in the Church of God and the convener of Qara: Church of God Women in Ministry, an organization for mobilizing and networking women clergy in the church. She holds a master's degree in leadership from Azusa Pacific University and a PhD in intercultural studies from Fuller Theological Seminary. MaryAnn is a sought-after speaker and teacher on leadership, mission, postmodern ministry and women in ministry.

Once more the preferred image, the home office, offers that all-important feature: nature. A big, clear window overlooks a lush, park-like meadow. Yet again we see that Millennials are drawn to the great outdoors. Another important attraction of the office is its location: home. Modularity may be the cultural norm for Millennials, but many are drawn to the idea that life's pieces can be coordinated and coherent instead of further divided.

A significant minority, however, chose the executive-style office as a place they would like to work. Whether this reflects the desire for a high-level career or simply a preference for a traditionally appointed workspace is unclear. Either way, we can see that some Millennials aren't immune to the comforts of a high-backed leather chair—and the implied corner office.

In the arena of work, more than any other, the church could play a role young adults have not needed until now. Due to the forces of modularity discussed earlier, young (and not-so-young) adults need resources that would have previously been provided by an employer. These may include a place to work (and the Internet connections and office machines that go with it), opportunities to network and training programs to teach skills that would otherwise be learned in an entry-level job.

There is room for some churches to go beyond a shared co-work space and develop loan-a-tool services and even full-bore apprenticeships for skilled laborers, where older workers pass on their know-how to the next generation. White-collar workers aren't the only ones who are transitioning to a freelance model.

Many churches have casual common areas that could serve freelance workers, but as the images show, many Millennials would prefer more structure than what is commonly found in these spaces. How could you adapt your communal space to help young adults reconnect "work" with the rest of life?

CROSS-CULTURAL COMMUNICATION

Millennials, like other people, don't always know how best to contend with the most significant areas of life. Some of them will turn to a community of faith for help. But the help they need and the help churches are accustomed to giving aren't always the same.

Consider your church's cultural expression of discipleship. If your standard Bible-teaching method is a 30- to 45-minute sermon delivered once a week by one leader on a stage at the front of your worship space, you may find it difficult not only to pass on rich Bible knowledge but merely to hold Millennials' attention. In fact, you may find it hard to hold Millennials' attention even if that's *not* your standard teaching method! If so, you're not alone. We asked our field groups in Chicago and Atlanta their theories for why churches have a hard time getting and keeping their attention. One young woman responded, "It's not just churches. It's everyone."

She's right. Facebook, NBC, Honda, political campaigns, nonprofits—these

Millennials need wisdom— spiritual understanding that allows them to put knowledge into practice.

organizations are all asking the same questions that are on churches' minds: how to attract and retain Millennial engagement. And even though few of these are in direct competition with churches for young adults' loyalty, the endless barrage of advertising, special offers, viral videos, ultimate listicles, can't-miss opportunities and promises of fulfillment is a formidable rival to any church's attempt to engage Millennials. Cognitive psychologists tell us humans can only focus on seven or so chunks of information at any one time (neuroscience suggests it may be even fewer). That is insufficient bandwidth to process the sheer volume of data that demands our attention each day. While some Millennials are actively screening out church, many who would be open to engaging with a faith community are simply too mentally overloaded to tune in—especially if that church adds to the noise and chaos instead of equipping young adults to make sense of it.

This leads us back to *cultural discernment*, which we touched on in the Introduction. Few Millennials need more information, from churches or anyone else. They have access to more knowledge than any generation in history. No, what they need is *wisdom*—spiritual understanding that allows them to put knowledge into practice. And churches, rooted in Scripture and alive in the Spirit, are in a singular position to train young disciples in the fine art of wisdom.

By way of example, here are two ways a church could engage in wisdom training.

First, is your community of faith equipping Millennials to be wise about digital tools? They are more likely than average to say they check their phone first thing in the morning (56% vs. 40% of all adults; see Figure 1.1) and last thing before bed (54% vs. 33%). They are also twice as likely than the national norm to check it in the middle of the night (12% vs. 6%). Beyond the brute facts of tech compulsion, half of Millennials agree, "My personal electronics sometimes separate me from other people" (49%). More than half say, "There are times when I think I have too much information" (56%). Young adults are more likely than average to say they felt physically or mentally overwhelmed five or more times during the past month (25% vs. 21% of all adults).

Our priorities, when it comes to young people and digital technology, often focus on avoiding ungodly content such as pornography—and, since porn consumption even among Christians is shockingly high, those efforts are a necessary response to our times. But a list of don'ts isn't wisdom. Many Millennials are seeking a more holistic, cohesive approach to tech—an approach that is fully integrated with the Christian understanding of what it means to be created in God's image.

Is your community of faith thinking deeply about these issues? Are you mentoring young adults toward wise use of technology that connects good teaching with godly practice?

• How does your business or organization make space within your culture for the next generation—and how could you leverage Millennials' cultural prefernces toward accomplishing your mission?

• In what ways does modularity impact your Millennial employees, stakeholders or customers—and what can you do to stay nimble and responsive to their changing needs?

• How is your organization contributing to or easing our cultural glut of "wisdomless" information—and how might a shift in your communications strategy tip the balance in favor of cultural discernment?

▶ 1.5   THE SOCIAL ISSUES

SELF-IDENTIFIED CHRISTIAN MILLENNIALS DON'T ALWAYS COME TO THE SAME CONCLUSIONS AS OLDER
GENERATIONS ABOUT MORALS AND VALUES.

ON SOME ISSUES MILLENNIALS TEND TO BE MORE CONSERVATIVE.
PLEASE INDICATE WHETHER YOU CONSIDER THE FOLLOWING ACTIVITY TO BE MORALLY ACCEPTABLE.

LIVING WITH SOMEONE OF THE OPPOSITE
SEX WITHOUT BEING MARRIED,
SOMETIMES CALLED COHABITATION

LOOKING AT PICTURES THAT DISPLAY
NUDITY OR EXPLICIT SEXUAL BEHAVIOR

ENJOYING SEXUAL THOUGHTS OR
FANTASIES ABOUT SOMEONE

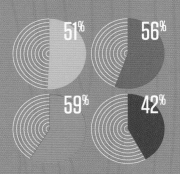

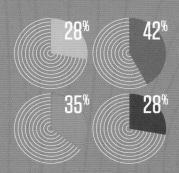

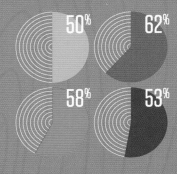

HAVING AN ABORTION

USING DRUGS THAT HAVE NOT BEEN
PRESCRIBED BY A MEDICAL DOCTOR

USING MARIJUANA FOR
RECREATIONAL USE

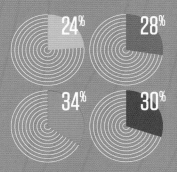

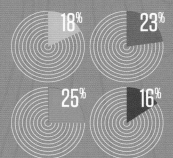

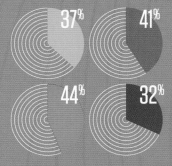

 MILLENNIALS   GEN-XERS   BOOMERS   ELDERS

AND ON SOME THEY ARE MORE LIBERAL.
DO YOU AGREE OR DISAGREE WITH THE FOLLOWING STATEMENTS?

USING PROFANITY

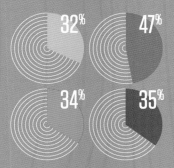

32%   47%

34%   35%

ANY UNION BETWEEN TWO MEN
OR TWO WOMEN SHOULD NOT BE
RECOGNIZED AS A LEGAL MARRIAGE.
(% DISAGREE)

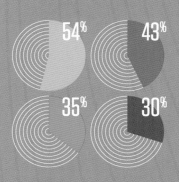

54%   43%

35%   30%

HOMOSEXUALS SHOULD BE ALLOWED TO
ADOPT CHILDREN. (% AGREE)

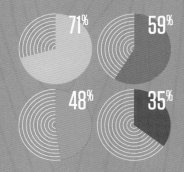

71%   59%

48%   35%

HOMOSEXUALS SHOULD BE ALLOWED TO
OPENLY SERVE IN THE MILITARY. (% AGREE)

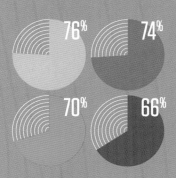

76%   74%

70%   66%

Second, there seems to be a lot of confusion, among Christians of all generations, about what it means to be Christlike. How should following Jesus affect our beliefs and behaviors?

Leading up to the release of his book *Mud and the Masterpiece*, John Burke, pastor of Gateway Church in Austin, Texas, wanted to find out if American Christians today are more like Jesus in action and attitude or more like the Pharisees, religious leaders of Jesus' time who often seemed more concerned with following the rules for being God's people than with actually *being* God's people. To assess Christ-likeness and Pharisee-likeness in their beliefs and behaviors, Barna designed a series of 20 questions to ask a representative panel of self-identified Christians. A numerical scale was used to tease out four distinct segments—Christians who are:

- Christlike in attitude and in action
- Pharisaical in attitude but Christlike in action
- Christlike in attitude but Pharisaical in action
- Pharisaical in attitude and in action

The bad news is that about half of self-identified Christians (51%) fall into the last category: Pharisaical in mindset and in behaviors. The good news? Your faith community can help.

Wisdom, guided by God's Spirit, is what allows us to connect right attitude with right action. But teaching young disciples *what* to think and *what* to do will not impart wisdom. We must train them (and relearn for ourselves) *how* to think and act like Jesus—to discern the right way to go and then to get going.

We should prepare ourselves for the real possibility that, if we older sisters and brothers in the faith do our job right, they may come up with different cultural expressions of the "what to think" and "what to do" questions. For example, as part of the Barna FRAMES project, we examined the differences between generations when it comes to social issues (see Figure 1.5). Practicing Christians under 40 are more likely than practicing Christians over 40 to favor legal recognition of rights and protections for gay and lesbian Americans (45% vs. 34%), and to agree that LGBT Americans should be allowed to adopt children (54% vs. 38%) and serve in the military without having to hide their sexual orientation (73% vs. 64%).

Should Christians in older generations be worried? Not if we are engaged, along with the next generation, in real-world, rubber-meets-the-road cultural discernment. Jesus promised his disciples, "When the Spirit of truth comes, he will lead you into all truth" (John 16:13, NLT). We trust this Spirit still today.

KINGDOM CULTURE

Perhaps the hardest thing about following Christ in a particular place, time and culture is separating our worldview assumptions about what is good from what God says is good. Every Christian community over the past two millennia has struggled with this tension, starting with the very first generation of believers.

Acts 15 recounts the culture clash between Jewish Jesus-followers and Gentile Jesus-followers. The Jewish believers naturally felt that male Gentile converts should be circumcised and all converts should be required to follow the Law of Moses. This made perfect sense within their worldview framework—after all, Jesus himself was circumcised and followed the Law!

But Peter, Paul and Barnabas, who were Jewish missionary-preachers to non-Jews, objected. Their objections were based on firsthand witness of the Holy Spirit at work among those who did not share Jewish values, allegiances and assumptions. It was clear to them that God makes "no distinction between us and them, for he cleansed their hearts through faith. . . . we are all saved the same way, by the undeserved grace of the Lord Jesus" (Acts 15:9,11). If God was prepared to save people from *outside* the Jewish worldview, it was wrong to insist that the new believers adopt cultural expressions from *inside* it.

The rest of the Jerusalem Council, the leaders of the fledgling Jesus community, were persuaded that their cultural norms should not be imposed on new Gentile converts. *But* . . . they also instructed new believers in Antioch to "abstain from eating food offered to idols, from consuming blood or the meat of strangled animals, and from sexual immorality" (Acts 15:29). These activities were entirely acceptable to non-Jewish worldview sensibilities. By asking Gentile believers to give up these cultural expressions, the early church leaders were, in essence, creating brand-new cultural norms for the Christian community.

Not Jewish culture. Not Gentile culture. Kingdom culture.

Paul wrote, "There is no longer Jew or Gentile, slave or free, male and female. For you are all one in Christ Jesus" (Gal. 3:28). In a similar way, the Jesus community today is called to transcend, with the Spirit's help, our generational values, allegiances and assumptions and adopt a shared Kingdom culture.

NOTE:

[1] Charles H. Kraft, *Anthropology for Christian Witness* (Maryknoll, NY: Orbis Books, 2013).

Richard Clark is Co-Founder and Editor-in-Chief of Christ & Pop Culture, *an online magazine that exists to acknowledge, appreciate and think rightly about the common knowledge of our age. He is also the managing editor of* Gamechurch *and a freelance writer for* Unwinnable *and* Paste, *among others. He lives with his wife in Louisville, Kentucky, and has an MA in Theology and the Arts from Southern Baptist Theological Seminary.*

What was the impetus behind creating *Christ & Pop Culture*? Why do you think cultural engagement is so important?

We want to help people understand that they're living in the midst of culture, that they're already engaging with it. Whether or not they acknowledge it or want to acknowledge it, pop culture is something they're engaging. The question is not whether we *should* engage culture, but whether we're doing it actively or passively. We want to encourage people to actively engage culture—whether that's in a positive or negative sense.

We focus on an appreciation of culture because we see that evangelicals, in particular, have done really well in terms of negative feedback. That's where our primary focus has been—sometimes for good effect and sometimes not. So a big part of our goal is to talk just as much about the positive things in culture. We believe negative engagement with culture

is most valuable when it's coupled with positive, active engagement.

What do you see as the biggest barrier or problem for churches and other faith organizations when it comes to their culture? What are some ways to overcome this hurdle?

A lot of twentysomethings are reacting to that negative engagement that the church has traditionally participated in. They see a need for positive engagement with culture, for the church to demonstrate how we can be actively engaged with culture in a way that's not separatist in some way or super negative. They are looking for people to model positive engagement.

The thing that worries me is the tendency to want to embrace everything and to be seen, in the eyes of the world, as positive and accepting. That impulse sometimes results in negative pushback against other cultures, particularly against previous generations of believers. So the desire to be accepted in the wider culture can have damaging effects in terms of Christian community.

What are the best practices you could recommend to churches or organizations that are considering how to train teens and young adults in wise cultural discernment?

It's not the same for all churches, obviously, but one of the key things is for leaders to know their congregation. You have to know people if you want to challenge them without alienating them in a needless way. Too many leaders either pander—like trying to be super relevant or cool and do all the trendy things for Millennials—or attack needlessly and pointlessly.

If you have a community with a lot of twentysomethings that are really into movies, bring the discussion they're already having into sermons or Sunday School or small groups. You have to be careful not to make it too formal, as if we're going to talk about a certain movie and all agree together what it means. Reactions to art are subjective and made on an individual level. People react to sin portrayed in mainstream movies—or even thoughtful "grace-filled" films—in specific, individual ways. And people's individual reactions are each valid responses. Don't start a class to tell people what to think about specific movies. It's not about *what* but *how*. Model how to engage with films. Talk about the underlying message of the movie. Discuss the reasons we all react differently. Dialog about what sins the movie exposes. In the past, if we watched a movie that caused us to covet, we'd say, "I need to stop watching movies." But a more valuable question is, "Why is that film causing me to covet?" Art can cause us to confront ourselves, which can lead to repentance.

Like it or not—and there are plenty of reasons not to, many of which are biblical—consumer culture has shaped what people expect of church and how some churches approach ministry.

It's tempting to think of church as one part of the "religious services industry"—the sector of the economy that provides spiritual goods and experiences to consumers. When we conceive of our faith community this way, even unconsciously, we understand our difficulty appealing to Millennials as a failure to create brand loyalty—a failure whose solution is a better product and / or better marketing. To be successful in our industry, we have to compete in a marketplace undergoing massive disruption as a generation of young consumers becomes ever more knowledgeable and selective about what they do and don't want, and has the technological savvy to cherry-pick from a variety of "service providers" if they can't find just one that meets all their unique, highly individualized needs.

If a ministry is successful, we assume, the people whom we serve will gradually become more deeply involved (that is, more loyal to our brand). For instance, if 200 children from the neighborhood attend Vacation Bible School but none of the kids or their parents comes to a church service after VBS is done, we would question whether VBS is an effective ministry. And it's a valid question—we should assess our ministry effectiveness early and often.

But we should also take a further step back to assess both our objectives and our metrics of success. Should the goal of our programs and ministries always be more people actively engaged in our programs and ministries? Is our mission to expand market share and brand loyalty?

It's such a powerful underlying assumption that we've developed an entire vocabulary to describe the ideal progression. "Onramps" and "entry points" lead to "assimilation" and "affiliation." Our community ministries are onramps that channel people from completely uninvolved to loyal attenders, givers and volunteers—who keep the onramps operating smoothly to reach more potential

Like it or not, consumer culture has shaped what people expect of church.

attenders, givers and volunteers.

If the church were just another business seeking market share, this frame of mind would be harmless or even beneficial. But the church is not. Our worshipping communities are nothing less than repositories of God's Spirit, continuing as his Body the work of redemption and restoration inaugurated in Christ.

There is good news: Many of the very people we are trying to reach—

▶ Q&A WITH JON TYSON

Jon Tyson is a church planter and lead pastor of Trinity Grace Church in New York City. He is also on the board of directors of the Origins Movement, a new church planting movement committed to multiplying missional church communities in the major urban centers of the world.

The top reason people give us for why they don't attend church is they find God elsewhere. When you hear that kind of reasoning—that God is available and findable outside of church—how do you respond?
It's too simplistic. There are three kinds of spirituality: mono-, di- and tri-spirituality. Mono-spirituality is what I would call secular spirituality. It basically says, *Secularism isn't working. There has to be more to me than just chemicals and brainwaves; I will look for a spiritual force or god within myself.* That sort of spirituality is a cloaking mechanism to stop you from having to depend on God.

Then you've got di-spirituality, which basically says, *No, I need something outside of myself. I need a relationship with a deity of some kind.* And this, I think, is often where evangelicalism goes wrong. Everything exists so I can have a personal relationship with God. Relationships with other people are incidental or secondary.

Tri-spirituality is myself in relationship with God *and* in relationship with others. This is the spirituality Jesus taught.

I think people are deluding themselves to think that outside of the body of believers—and I say "body" deliberately,

not church programs or Sunday events—that outside of the Body of Jesus Christ, people can find God. You will have a limited, immature, shallow spirituality if you think you can find it on your own. We are called to practice the way of Jesus with other people.

My guess, though, is what people are really saying is they find church mediocre—that it's about guilt, condemnation and hypocrisy. They want to live the faith outside of that pattern.

If people get together regularly with a big group of friends to live the way of Jesus, *and* if they're laying down their lives in sacrificial love, they're doing church. In my experience, though, most people who don't want to "go to church" don't get around to the second part.

You have suggested the drivers of consumer-oriented church are not just the consumer—the individual churchgoer—and the culture, but also the leader's expectations for what it means to be a community of faith. How can leaders avoid falling into the trap of becoming a consumer-driven church?
I think the issue is what evangelical culture focuses on as success and holds up as the model of success. Every

Millennials—are hyperaware and deeply suspicious of the intersection of church and consumer culture. This doesn't mean they're not avid consumers, for most certainly are. But many also have a sense that church should be different somehow, above or beyond the dirty business of sell, sell, sell.

Their reluctance to buy what we're selling is good news because it gives us a chance to decide if we are, in fact, different somehow. Are we more concerned with making the sale than with making disciples?

conference you attend, the speakers are, for the most part, charismatic, disproportionately gifted, un-reproducible anomalies. And they lead churches that are, for the most part, in unique contexts at unique cultural moments that cannot be scaled or multiplied easily. We hold up the anomaly and try to make it the expectation. We live in an evangelical culture that robs us of our pastoral joy by repeatedly telling us to compare ourselves to people we can never be.

Very practically, pastors must first claim a biblical definition of success and root it in our hearts. According to the Bible, success is *faithfulness*: "Well done, good and faithful servant."

So, number one, we need to have a vision of faithfulness as true, biblical success. Number two, we must sacrificially lay down our lives in love—which means focusing on the relationships that are actually before us and asking the question, *How can I more tangibly manifest the love of Jesus in the actual relationships God has brought to me?* And number three, we must keep our lives focused on the needs of the world rather than striving for success or notoriety in any sort of ecclesiological platform. Celebrity and consumerism go hand in hand.

What would be your advice to a Millennial pastor who is dealing personally with the culture of distraction? Or to a Boomer pastor who's trying to reach Millennials?
Our culture of distraction is unprecedented in human history. And the challenge of getting people to focus, to be still, to walk with God, to hear from God, to think and read and have convictions on any sort of deep level, is just incredibly hard.

To a Boomer pastor I would say, offer the gifts you have from your own story, journey and experience—so another generation doesn't have to make those same mistakes. People are craving mentors to give them wisdom on how to live. I think there should be a massive increase in terms of mentoring—that's an incredible gift Boomers can give.

To a Millennial pastor, I would simply say, follow the path of wisdom, not the path of trends. We can't let all these intrusions continually make their way into our lives. We have to put boundaries in place. In some sense, *silence, solitude* and *stopping* are the essential disciplines a Millennial pastor has to practice.

• How well does
your welcome /
hospitality ministry
respect and respond
to outsiders—and
what could you do
differently to defer
social status to your
guests?

• Do your programs
and events foster
life-shaping,
intergenerational
relationships—and
what kind of training
or resourcing do older
adults need to invest
more deeply in the
lives of teens and
young adults?

• Do people
encounter Jesus when
they join with your
faith community—
and how can you
better orient various
ministries toward
bringing people closer
to him?

CLOSED DOORS

So what do Millennials think about church? Why have so many closed the door on church involvement? Why, even among those who grew up in church, have nearly six in 10 dropped out at some point? Why have more than half been absent from church for the past six months? Why do three in 10 Millennials say church is not at all important while an additional four in 10 feel ambivalent, saying church is either somewhat important or somewhat not important?

In Barna's research for the FRAMES series, we asked Millennials why they do or don't think church is important. Their answers reveal a general feeling that church is simply not necessary—and, for some, that it is harmful.

Among those who say church is not important, most are split between two reasons: Two in five say church isn't important because they can find God elsewhere (39%), and one-third say it's because church is not personally relevant to them (35%). One in three simply find church boring (31%) and one in five say it feels like God is missing from church (20%). Only 8% say they don't attend because church is "out of date," undercutting the notion that all we need to do for Millennials is to make church "cooler."

A significant number of young adults have deeper complaints about church. More than one-third say their negative perceptions are a result of moral failures in church leadership (35%). And substantial majorities of Millennials who don't go to church say they see Christians as judgmental (87%), hypocritical (85%), anti-homosexual (91%) and insensitive to others (70%).

We asked participants in the Barna / CKN national survey to rate how well each statement in a series describes the Christian community in America. Fewer than half of respondents agree a lot or somewhat that the statement "The people at church are tolerant of those with different beliefs" describes the church (46%). About the same proportion say that "The church seems too much like an exclusive club" is an accurate description (44%). Taken together, a significant number of young adults perceive a lack of relational generosity within the U.S. Christian community.

More worrisome are the two-thirds of Millennials who believe American churchgoers are a lot or somewhat hypocritical (66%). To a generation that prides itself on the ability to smell a fake at 10 paces, hypocrisy is the mother of all indictments.

These negative perceptions are not limited to word descriptions. When asked to select the image that best represents "present-day Christianity," Millennials show the same basic pattern.

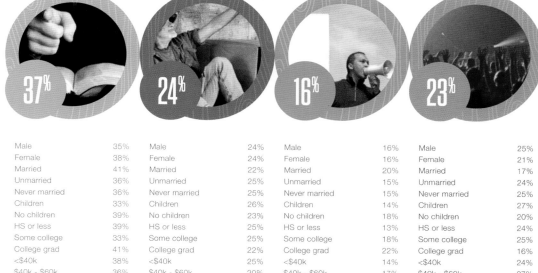

	37%		24%		16%		23%
Male	35%	Male	24%	Male	16%	Male	25%
Female	38%	Female	24%	Female	16%	Female	21%
Married	41%	Married	22%	Married	20%	Married	17%
Unmarried	36%	Unmarried	25%	Unmarried	15%	Unmarried	24%
Never married	36%	Never married	25%	Never married	15%	Never married	25%
Children	33%	Children	26%	Children	14%	Children	27%
No children	39%	No children	23%	No children	18%	No children	20%
HS or less	39%	HS or less	25%	HS or less	13%	HS or less	24%
Some college	33%	Some college	25%	Some college	18%	Some college	25%
College grad	41%	College grad	22%	College grad	22%	College grad	16%
<$40k	38%	<$40k	25%	<$40k	14%	<$40k	24%
$40k - $60k	36%	$40k - $60k	20%	$40k - $60k	17%	$40k - $60k	27%
$60k+	36%	$60k+	26%	$60k+	18%	$60k+	20%
Churched	28%	Churched	35%	Churched	8%	Churched	30%
Marginally churched	42%	Marginally churched	22%	Marginally churched	9%	Marginally churched	27%
Unchurched	41%	Unchurched	19%	Unchurched	22%	Unchurched	18%
Other faith	40%	Other faith	13%	Other faith	28%	Other faith	19%
No faith	41%	No faith	10%	No faith	29%	No faith	21%
White	36%	White	26%	White	18%	White	21%
Black	42%	Black	16%	Black	10%	Black	33%
Hispanic	39%	Hispanic	23%	Hispanic	16%	Hispanic	22%
Nonwhite	39%	Nonwhite	22%	Nonwhite	14%	Nonwhite	25%
Northeast	38%	Northeast	25%	Northeast	15%	Northeast	22%
South	38%	South	28%	South	17%	South	17%
Midwest	41%	Midwest	20%	Midwest	16%	Midwest	24%
West	28%	West	27%	West	18%	West	27%

Barna/CKN, October 2013, N=843 U.S. adults ages 18 to 29 years old. The segmentation percentages above are among Millennials who participated in the study.

A majority—from all faith backgrounds, including Christianity—chose one of the two negative images. More than one-third chose the pointing finger (37%), and another one in six chose the bullhorn-wielding protestor (16%). In total, 52% of respondents view present-day Christianity as aggressive and critical.

But the perceptions are not all negative. About one in four chose the crowd of worshippers (23%). (Exiles—young adults who feel caught between culture and the church's expectations—were more likely than average to resonate with this image.) Some may have chosen the worshippers because they see Christianity as vibrant and communal (among practicing Christians, 31% chose this picture),

▶ Q&A WITH KATHY KHANG

Kathy Khang is the multiethnic director for InterVarsity Christian Fellowship Great Lakes West region. She is a coauthor of More Than Serving Tea, *which explores faith, gender, culture and ethnic identity from the perspective of Asian American Christian women, and was one of the activists behind the "Asian American Open Letter to the Evangelical Church." She is a regular speaker at colleges and conferences and lives with her husband, Peter Chang, in the north suburbs of Chicago with their three children, Bethany, Corban and Elias.*

How do the nationally representative findings sync with what you see among ethnic minority communities of faith? Are Millennial attitudes, beliefs and practices related to faith and church different in minority groups? In young first-generation Americans? Or do you see similar trends to the national study?

According to various studies of Christian Millennials, including Barna and others, more than half of them are people of color. But since non-white segments are small compared to the white majority, it's easy to assume there is a rush out the church doors across the board. "The Millennials are leaving! The Millennials are leaving!" Yes—but it's mostly white Millennials who identify as "nones," those with no religious ties.

America's diversity offers the church opportunities for growth. There are countless non-white Millennials who are more likely than their white counterparts to stay connected to church and to put down deep roots in their faith and neighborhood communities. But if we rely on a mostly white (and male) leadership to develop and implement strategies for outreach, evangelism and

discipleship to this diverse generation, these initiatives are more likely to fail.

One response is the emergence and growth of multiethnic congregations for whom diversity is a distinct feature of their mission. Millennials and Gen-Xers appear to be fueling the growth of these churches, but I have observed that there's sometimes a disconnect between the ethnic and racial experiences of older church leaders and those realities for younger church members. For example, second-generation American Millennials often have quite a different ethnic or racial identity process than first-generation immigrants, whether Millennial or older. Or Millennials of color may not connect in the same way with stories of the civil rights era as previous generations who lived it. The perspectives of church leaders who came up in the time of language-immersion programs and Jim Crow laws are understandably shaped by those experiences. Millennials of color, particularly those in college or with college degrees, have come of age under a politically correct diversity that may have limited their personal experience of racism—so far.

and others because they view Christianity as emotional and consumer-oriented. In other words, this image might have been selected because it resonates with either negative or positive connotations for different Millennials.

One in four chose the overtly positive image, the helping hand reaching out to a person in need (24%). It's encouraging that a significant proportion of Millennials view Christianity this way. The percentage is even higher among practicing Christian young adults (34%), indicating that those who are engaged in a local church want to live out a faith that is actively reaching into their community.

These factors and more impact how young adults do or do not connect with a church pursuing multiethnicity.

To bridge these divides, leaders who want to plant or develop an intentionally multiethnic community of faith should use illustrations, images and applications that do not solely focus on historic, systemic racism or ethnic prejudice but that also connect history to more recent examples of injustice.

White leaders, including pastors and lay leaders, should put themselves under the mentoring of leaders of color who are living out the generational transition in their congregations and families. How many leaders attend big Christian leadership conferences but never connect in a significant way with the Hispanic or Asian American pastor whose congregation rents the building on Sunday afternoons? How many church leaders read the latest leadership books but have never been in a church that is significantly different in its ethnicity, denomination or location?

I suggest developing partnerships between the local congregation, on-campus parachurch organizations and community organizers.

This season of life—college through young professional adult—is easily disconnected from the local church because of geography and time. Churches not located within walking distance of campus may not often see Millennial visitors—never mind that 8 or 10 a.m. Sunday is not the most active time, especially for undergraduates. But parachurch organizations are already on campus, positioned to fit the schedules of undergrads and even graduates and young professionals. Imagine the relational networks that could be built between older generations at church and on-campus Millennials who want to be mentored.

In addition to campus parachurch organizations, churches should build connections with local community organizers. These folks are concerned with making the lives of those in the neighborhood better—and Millennials, nearly across the board, are concerned with the way faith is lived out holistically, daily and locally.

Connecting young adults to a community's future invites them to put down roots and invest themselves over the long haul.

30%

SAY ATTENDING CHURCH
IS NOT AT ALL IMPORTANT

40%

FALL SOMEWHERE
IN THE MIDDLE

30%

SAY ATTENDING CHURCH
IS VERY IMPORTANT

THOSE WHO SAY CHURCH ATTENDANCE IS NOT IMPORTANT
POINT TO THE FOLLOWING REASONS ...

THOSE WHO SAY CHURCH ATTENDANCE IS VERY IMPORTANT
POINT TO THE FOLLOWING REASONS ...

39% "I FIND GOD ELSEWHERE"

35% "IT'S NOT RELEVANT TO ME"

31% "CHURCH IS BORING"

20% "IT FEELS LIKE GOD IS MISSING FROM CHURCH"

8% "CHURCH FEELS OUT OF DATE"

4% "I DON'T LIKE THE PEOPLE"

"I GO TO BE CLOSER TO GOD" **44%**

"I LEARN ABOUT GOD THERE" **27%**

"THE BIBLE SAYS TO GO" **22%**

"MY KIDS LEARN ABOUT GOD THERE" **13%**

"THE CHURCH DOES GOOD WORK IN THE WORLD" **8%**

"MY FRIENDS ARE THERE" **5%**

AMONG ALL MILLENNIALS

66%
AMERICAN
CHURCHGOERS ARE
HYPOCRITICAL

46%
PEOPLE AT CHURCH ARE
TOLERANT OF THOSE
WITH DIFFERENT BELIEFS

44%
THE CHURCH SEEMS
TOO MUCH LIKE AN
EXCLUSIVE CLUB

65%
CHURCH IS A PLACE TO
FIND ANSWERS TO LIVE A
MEANINGFUL LIFE

54%
CHURCH IS
RELEVANT
FOR MY LIFE

49%
I CAN
"BE MYSELF"
AT CHURCH

If those are the closed doors of negative views on the church, positive perceptions are windows that show Millennials' openness to connecting with the Jesus community. What do they find valuable in church? Their answers can give us insights for what to prioritize in ministry to and with Millennials.

A plurality say they attend church to be closer to God (44%) and nearly three in 10 go to learn more about God (27%). Getting outside the humdrum of their everyday lives to experience transcendence—in worship, in prayer, in teaching—is a key desire for many Millennials when it comes to church.

Two-thirds of survey participants say a good description of church is "a place to find answers to live a meaningful life" (a lot + somewhat = 65%). Over half say "church is relevant for my life" (54%), and about half "feel I can 'be myself' at church" (49%). Three out of five survey respondents say it is not true that "the faith and teaching I encounter at church seem rather shallow" (not too much + not at all = 62%), and about the same number would not agree with the statement "the church is not a safe place to express doubts" (60%).

That's a lot of open windows.

We asked Millennials to select an aspirational image for what church should be in the world and found that, by and large, young adults respect the potential of organized religion (see Figure 2.3). Almost half chose the image of a small-group Bible study (48%), combining the social and intellectual aspects of Christianity. Most of the rest chose the image of a growing flower (33%), which implies the possibility of personal growth and for cultivating beauty. The other two images—the hospital and the health club—were much less popular (12% and 7%, respectively). Still, these metaphors are meaningful to many Millennials.

	48%		7%		12%		33%
Male	48%	Male	10%	Male	12%	Male	30%
Female	48%	Female	4%	Female	13%	Female	36%
Married	43%	Married	5%	Married	16%	Married	37%
Unmarried	49%	Unmarried	8%	Unmarried	11%	Unmarried	32%
Never married	50%	Never married	8%	Never married	12%	Never married	30%
Children	51%	Children	7%	Children	12%	Children	30%
No children	45%	No children	7%	No children	12%	No children	35%
HS or less	51%	HS or less	7%	HS or less	11%	HS or less	31%
Some college	48%	Some college	8%	Some college	11%	Some college	33%
College grad	41%	College grad	6%	College grad	17%	College grad	36%
<$40k	47%	<$40k	6%	<$40k	13%	<$40k	33%
$40k - $60k	53%	$40k - $60k	7%	$40k - $60k	6%	$40k - $60k	34%
$60k+	46%	$60k+	8%	$60k+	14%	$60k+	32%
Churched	58%	Churched	5%	Churched	12%	Churched	26%
Marginally churched	46%	Marginally churched	3%	Marginally churched	25%	Marginally churched	26%
Unchurched	42%	Unchurched	9%	Unchurched	10%	Unchurched	39%
Other faith	32%	Other faith	9%	Other faith	9%	Other faith	50%
No faith	29%	No faith	6%	No faith	17%	No faith	48%
White	42%	White	9%	White	17%	White	10%
Black	64%	Black	3%	Black	6%	Black	19%
Hispanic	55%	Hispanic	10%	Hispanic	5%	Hispanic	10%
Nonwhite	57%	Nonwhite	8%	Nonwhite	5%	Nonwhite	12%
Northeast	49%	Northeast	6%	Northeast	14%	Northeast	31%
South	43%	South	9%	South	10%	South	38%
Midwest	53%	Midwest	5%	Midwest	13%	Midwest	29%
West	43%	West	9%	West	11%	West	37%

Barna/CKN, October 2013, N=843 U.S. adults ages 18 to 29 years old. The segmentation percentages above are among Millennials who participated in the study.

What can we conclude overall? Millennials are, on the whole, skeptical about the role churches play in society. This is the closed door. But their hope for the role churches *could* play? That's an open window.

What do these findings mean for how we make space for Millennials in our ministries?

What do you see as the biggest barrier or problem for churches and faith organizations when it comes to Millennials' perceptions? What are some ways to overcome this hurdle?
Many Millennials perceive the church to be judgmental, out-of-touch and riddled with political striving. They see the church as an institution structured to meet its own internal goals: attendance, souls saved, financial obligations. They also see the church as largely disconnected from the day-to-day lives of people and neighborhoods.

With C. Christopher Smith, I wrote *Slow Church: Cultivating Community in the Patient Way of Jesus.* Slow Church is inspired by Slow Food and other Slow movements to rethink the ways we share life together in our church communities. Slow Food views consumers as active participants in production. An eater who knows where her food comes from, knows how it got to her table and supports local farmers is nothing less than a co-producer.

Millennials want to be a part of something. They hear about a Jesus revolution, but what they find in churches is something like drive-thru faith, a Sunday morning pit stop you make on the way to wherever you're really going. The American church is just as susceptible as the rest of culture to the allure of "Fast Life." We get wrapped up, for example, in finding the most efficient, predictable, countable and controllable way to get someone from here to there—from unsaved to saved, from unchurched to churched. When the values of "McDonaldization" replace

faithfulness as the standard by which we evaluate life in our churches, it's easy to justify cookie-cutter approaches to disciple making. Ministries churn out Christians notable not for their authentic peculiarity but for their bland sameness.

"Taste and see that the Lord is good," says the psalmist. As we follow Jesus together, we experience in new ways the complex palate of God's goodness. Similarly, since the church is the Body of Christ, it is partly through the church that the world tastes God. This is why we can't sacrifice quality to quantity.

Rather than confining the life of faith to Sunday mornings where it can be kept safe and predictable, or to a "personal relationship with Jesus Christ" that can be managed from the privacy of our own home, ministry should cultivate a deep, holistic discipleship that touches every aspect of our lives. Following Jesus isn't a privatized faith, but rather a lifelong apprenticeship undertaken in Christian community.

Reading through the results of this research, what strikes me is not how different Millennials are from you and me, but how similar. They seem to want what we all wanted once upon a time: wholeness, a life that hasn't been bifurcated into the spiritual and the non-spiritual.

Whether or not they can be persuaded to darken the door of a church building, my Millennial Christian friends want to be a part of God's reconciling mission. A ministry's perspective on this point—"Is our goal to create passive consumers of religious goods and services, or to empower co-participants in God's

John Pattison is the co-author of Slow Church: Cultivating Community in the Patient Way of Jesus *and* Besides the Bible: 100 Books that Have, Should, or Will Create Christian Culture*, both from InterVarsity Press. He is also the Managing Editor of* CONSPIRE *magazine. A member of the National Book Critics Circle, his essays, articles and reviews have also appeared in* Books & Culture, RELEVANT *magazine, as part of Powells.com's Review-a-Day program and in newspapers and magazines around the country. He lives in Oregon's Mid-Willamette Valley with his wife and two daughters.*

reconciling mission?"—shapes how we reach out to Millennials. In the former, evangelism is recommending a favorite brand. In the latter, it is inviting others to join a Movement.

Joining the movement of God's kingdom involves attentiveness to what God is doing around us—attentiveness that is nurtured over time and in place. This is long, slow work. But what's so great is *everything matters*. Even the down times, the dailiness of apprenticing ourselves to Jesus, all the quotidian details of life, the smallest acts of hospitality or generosity—they are all woven together by God into the fabric of God's kingdom.

How does a "Slow Church" approach intersect (or contradict) our increasingly digital lives?

I have two areas of concern related to the digital life of the Millennial generation—and, increasingly, older and younger generations too.

First, we can't substitute "real time" for real life. Theologian Phil Kenneson has helped us see how all-important authentic presence is. What God wants to give us, he says, is God's presence. And God wants *our* presence. *And* the most precious gift we can give to another human being is our presence. But if we're not careful, if we migrate too much of our time and attention to digital technology, we are in danger of short-circuiting faithful presence. This is an area in which the church can embody a refreshing alternative to the culture at large—not being legalistic about technology, of course, but engaging as a community in practices that reconnect us to each other, to God, to the land

and to our own deeper selves: eating together, going on hikes or quiet walks, reading poetry, taking a technology Sabbath, and so on.

Second, we need to be part of communities we can't control. Social media is a curated community. We decide who to friend and un-friend, who to follow and to block. Nothing wrong with that. But one of the important things about joining a church and staying put is that we become part of a community of people largely not of our choosing. We talk in *Slow Church* about the virtue of "stability"—of making a commitment to people and place. There is always the temptation to pull up stakes when things get tough and go in search of greener pastures. But, as one Cistercian vow of stability puts it, "Ultimately there is no escape from oneself, and the idea that things would be better someplace else is usually an illusion. And when interpersonal conflicts arise, we have a great incentive to work things out and restore peace. This means learning the practices of love: acknowledging one's own offensive behavior, giving up one's preferences, forgiving."

What should be the goal of ministry? By what metrics of success should we measure our efforts?

The goal of ministry is deeper faithfulness to the Way of Jesus in community.

The emphasis in Scripture is not on numbers but on faithfulness, as when Jesus says in Luke 18:8, "When the Son of Man comes will he find faith on the earth?" The apostle Paul's primary concern was following well in the footsteps of Jesus and his integrity as "a minister of Christ Jesus to the Gentiles"

(Rom. 15:16). The two churches that get the highest praise in Revelation are Smyrna and Philadelphia, described respectively as being poor and having no influence (Rev. 2:8-11; 3:7-13).

And yet it can be hard to measure faithfulness, so we need to be more creative with our metrics of success, and we need to think more long-term. These measures might include:

How many children who grew up in the church have committed themselves to a church in college or as adults?

How many neighborhood groups are utilizing our facilities during the week?

How diverse is our congregation— economically, racially and ethnically, generationally, politically?

What did we learn from this ministry initiative or outreach effort?

I would also encourage your church to focus more on stories. Designate someone as your church's memory keeper, someone to record the stories of God's faithfulness in your church and neighborhood. Once a year, recite those stories, rehearse them together and remember God's abundant provision.

What are three to five tips or best practices you could offer to churches or organizations that are considering how to minister to and with Millennials?

First, I would encourage churches and organizations to focus on the "with" part of this question. I think Millennials sense that they are seen as prizes to be won. Instead, we need to recognize them for what they really are: vital members of the Body whose voice and vision are necessary to the healthy life of the church. Along the same lines, churches shouldn't ghettoize Millennials as an "age demographic." They should be engaging in the work of the church with those who are younger and older than they are.

Second, churches and faith-based organizations should create space for open, honest conversation. Learning to talk together well, rooted in our particular places, we learn to think and speak theologically in a distinctive vernacular that fits who and where we are. A conversational church values the gifts and wisdom God has provided its members and neighbors. If our goal is to move from being passive consumers of church to active participants in the mission of God in the world, decisions made without conversation are unlikely to be sustainable or truly formational.

Third, we should ask Millennials to help our churches engage in the life of our neighborhood—or to catalyze life if there's not much going on yet. Here are some things churches can do:

Create an "asset map" of your congregation and neighborhood. Pay particular attention to the gifts of those we tend to marginalize: the young and the old, those with physical or emotional challenges, and so on.

Carefully study the histories of your church and of its neighborhood. Where do those stories intersect?

Identify a few of the people, places, rhythms and shared beliefs that give your community its unique taste and texture. Talk about how your church can tease out some of the delicious flavors already present there.

Finally, churches should *play together*. Millennials—and our youngest kids, sometimes called Generation Z—can remind us how it's done.

• What are the
challenges for
Christian education
created by many
Millennials' negative
perceptions of
Christianity—and
what can you do to
overcome them?

• The image of
group Bible study
was chosen by half
of Millennials as
best representing
what church should
be; how do you see
Christian education
fitting with this
aspiration?

• What part do
intergenerational
relationships play
in your educational
approach—and how
could you make them
a greater priority?

RESPECT & RESPOND

Let's start our ministry assessment with how we make room for guests.

Social status is a universal cultural phenomenon. Every human culture in the history of the world has had people of higher status and lower status. What factors determine one's status varies widely from culture to culture, as do protocols for how to treat people of different statuses. However, there is one universal when it comes to social status: The person of higher status sets the terms of the relationship, and the person of lower status respects and responds to the boundaries set by the higher-status person.

Think back to your first job. Unless you worked for a small, family-owned business, you almost certainly did not invite the company president or CEO to your home for dinner—at least, not on your first day. (Saying "hello" in the hallway may even have been a stretch.) To do so would have violated the rules of social status. How presumptuous of you! But it wouldn't have been presumptuous at all for the head of the company to invite *you* to dinner. The higher-status person—in this case, the CEO—sets the boundaries of the relationship.

Many churches, in our efforts to be friendly and welcoming to visitors, unintentionally assume the higher-status role. We stick out our hands, leaving no choice but to shake or be rude. We request personal information, communicating that we're in a social position to do so.

As a rule, Millennials are not terribly status-conscious, but they *are* keenly aware that information is power. In our national survey of 18- to 29-year-olds, we asked what information they would be comfortable giving to a church when they visit. (Remember, with fewer than half of Millennials having attended church in the past six months, it's fair to say that if and when they go to church, it's usually as an outsider. Even those who are not strangers to church may feel like outsiders if it has been awhile since they attended.)

The only piece of information a sizeable majority of Millennials is comfortable sharing with your church is their first name (82%). Only half are willing to give their last names (53%). Just one-third are comfortable sharing their email address (33%). That means two out of three young-adult visitors do not want you to have that information.

"Great!" you might say. "Our visitor system is so out of date we don't even ask for email, only for a phone number and address." Unfortunately, that's even worse. Only one in five Millennials are comfortable handing over their physical address (19%), and even fewer their phone number (12%). A mere 6% are willing to grant you access on social media, such as friending on Facebook or following on Twitter or Instagram.

About one in six Millennials would rather not share anything (15%). Among non-Christian young adults, it's more than one in four (28%).

Millennials are generally not restrictive of their personal information and privacy, but they tend to distrust churches. In fact, according to research Barna conducted for our FRAMES series, Millennials are the least likely generation to say the church has their best interests at heart (30%, compared to 34% of Gen-Xers and 41% of Boomers and Elders). This is one reason they prefer to stay off your radar until they are comfortable with you.

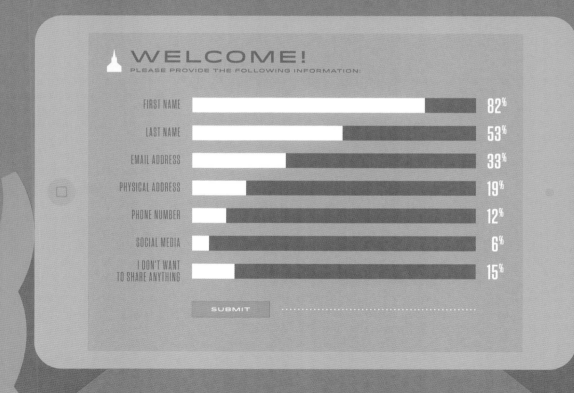

2.4 RESTRICTED ACCESS

MILLENNIALS ARE HESITANT TO SHARE MUCH INFORMATION WITH A CHURCH WHEN THEY VISIT FOR THE FIRST TIME:

WELCOME!
PLEASE PROVIDE THE FOLLOWING INFORMATION:

FIRST NAME	82%
LAST NAME	53%
EMAIL ADDRESS	33%
PHYSICAL ADDRESS	19%
PHONE NUMBER	12%
SOCIAL MEDIA	6%
I DON'T WANT TO SHARE ANYTHING	15%

SUBMIT

• How does your organization confer social status based on age—preferring those who are older or younger—and what are some ways you can respect and respond to all of your workers, volunteers or stakeholders?

• How do you see Millennials' negative and positive perceptions of the Christian community affecting your organization—and how could you play a part in tipping their perceptions toward the positive?

• How could your organization foster intergenerational relationships to help Millennials sustain their passion for your mission?

Ignoring visitors is not the solution, but consider how your church could defer social status to your guests. When Millennials visit your faith community, are they welcomed and respected, or harassed and put on the spot? Are they cornered into conversation or physical contact? Are they peppered with requests for personal information? Or are they free to set the boundaries of the relationship, as they feel comfortable?

Think about how you can respect and respond, rather than assert and demand. Perhaps a smile and a nod or wave from a greeter, rather than a handshake. Maybe a clearly marked welcome kiosk instead of someone intercepting them the minute they set foot in the door. Or an information card that is entirely optional, or with a checkbox to opt out of further contact. The leader who welcomes everyone to the worship service could communicate where, how and from whom to get more information, putting your guest in the driver's seat, socially speaking.

Taking control of the relationship makes sense if the endgame is to close a sale and create a loyal customer. But if our goal is to embody Christ's love, service and humility, we must take a different approach.

LIFE-SHAPING RELATIONSHIPS

Once our Millennial guests are through the door, basking in respectful and responsive hospitality, what do we do next?

In the Introduction, we touched on five reasons Millennials stay connected to church. As we saw in the first chapter about culture, engaging with young adults in cultural discernment is one of the ways churches train young disciples in wise, Jesus-shaped living. And in the chapter on leadership, we will explore how reverse mentoring and vocational discipleship make space for Millennial disciples in our leadership structures.

The remaining two reasons Millennials stay connected to church are the centerpiece of meaningful ministry to the next generation: *relationships* and *Jesus*.

Young adults who continue their involvement in a local church beyond their teen years are twice as likely as those who don't to have a close personal friendship with an older adult in their faith community (59% vs. 31% among church drop-outs). They're also twice as likely to have had a mentor other than a pastor or youth minister (28% vs. 11%). That means, conversely, that seven out of 10 Millennials who dropped out of church did not have a close friendship with an older adult, and nearly nine out of 10 never had a mentor at their church.

Of course, correlation does not equal causation. But if Jesus' discipling style is any indication, consistent, deepening friendship over a long period of time and through life's hills and valleys is an (if not *the*) essential element of lasting spiritual formation within the community of faith.

How well is your church or faith-based organization nurturing intergenerational friendships? Are you making space for generations to rub shoulders and share their hearts and minds, or are different age groups like East and West, never the twain shall meet? Are you cultivating ministries that encourage cross-pollination to breed a fresh harvest of Jesus followers? Are friendships flourishing that can sustain younger and older adults during seasons of spiritual dryness? Do Millennials—and everyone else—know they are relationally safe to explore doubts about God's goodness, questions about evil and suffering, and insecurities about their mission and calling in the world? Do people of all generations serve together, blessing their community with God's abundant grace and unconditional love?

Serving is not incidental for the next generation. Barna Group partnered with Compassion International to assess Americans' attitudes toward and perceptions of extreme global poverty. The study found that, among the general population, there is broad agreement that Christians have a unique obligation to the issue; two-thirds of U.S. adults agree strongly or somewhat that Christians should play a strong role in alleviating poverty (66%).

The proportion of practicing Christians under 40 who agree is even higher: nearly nine in 10 (86%). But that's not all. About half of young practicing Christians say their church should be more involved in fighting extreme poverty (47%), and almost the same number say they would give more if their church were more involved with poverty alleviation (45%). Among Millennials who attend church, one in six say it's important to them because the church is God's hands and feet in the world (16%).

Millennials have a reputation for being concerned about social justice, even though their record as effective, long-haul activists is spotty thus far. They share an expectation that communities of faith should lead the charge on justice issues like poverty. And when a church's resources are channeled inward instead of outward, they don't hesitate to criticize.

When our mobile focus groups in Chicago and Atlanta visited suburban megachurches, participants in both locations commented that such facilities must require a lot of financial resources to build and maintain. "It feels like a really big business," said one. "There's a lot of money here," another observed. Participants in both groups expressed skepticism and mistrust of a church that spends too much on itself instead of on serving others. (To be fair, both churches we visited have generous outreach and missions budgets, but these programs were not front and center to counteract the groups' impression of extravagance.) To Millennials, sacrificial generosity is non-negotiable when it comes to communities that claim to follow Jesus.

There is an aspirational element involved in this high standard—and isn't that a good thing? Many in the younger generation express a desire to make the world a better place. Their desire is a faint echo of God's intention to remake the heavens and the earth into a whole, healed place where he will dwell forever with his people (see Rev. 2:1-5). What would it look like for your church to mentor Millennials to live in the new creation? If young adults aspire to be sacrificially generous but don't know how, their mentoring friendships should incorporate clear teaching on and rigorous practice of the Christian virtue of charity.

MORE OF JESUS

Serving with a godly, trustworthy older friend isn't the only thing a young adult needs to stay connected to a family of faith. She should also be able to seek and find Jesus.

Sadly, one in five Millennials with a church background reports, "God seems missing from my experience of church" (20%). (This includes both dropouts and regular church attenders.) Among young adults who drop out of church involvement, just one in four believes Jesus speaks to them in a personal and relevant way, compared to seven out of 10 of those who remain in Christian community.

It's a chicken-or-egg question to identify if people drop out of church because they haven't heard from Jesus or if they haven't heard from Jesus because they're disconnected from church (or if the correlation of these two factors is merely coincidental). The fact remains that eight out of 10 young

▶ Q&A WITH SCOTT TODD

Scott Todd has been at Compassion for a decade and is currently the Senior Vice President for Global Advocacy. He is the author of Hope Rising: How Christians Can End Extreme Poverty in This Generation. *Dr. Todd is an award-winning scientist in Immunology and Oncology. He holds a doctorate from the University of California, a National Lymphoma Foundation fellowship at Stanford University Medical Center and numerous research grants.*

What are some best practices you could offer to churches or organizations that are considering how to minister to and with Millennials?

I suppose that for 2,000 years the perennial concern of the "middle generation" of Christians is whether those of the next generation will keep the faith. (And I wonder what it says of us that we do not survey our elders to learn whether they think our generation has kept the faith.) Compassion International works with over 1.5 million children and youth from cultures around the world. The expressions of Christian faith vary greatly from Korea to Uganda, from China to Nicaragua, and in every other diverse pocket of the human experience. I don't suppose it wise, or even possible, to paint with one brush the beliefs and desires of the Millennial generation of Americans— let alone the rest of the world. Yet I'm certain whatever Jesus had in mind when he founded the church must be

applicable in all these cultures and for all generations.

What did Jesus have in mind when he founded the church? Would Millennials, and the rest of us, answer favorably to whatever Jesus wanted the church to be? I believe they, and we, would be split—of two minds—in our answers. Ask Millennials if they value connection, relationship and belonging and their answer will be yes. Ask Millennials if they are tired of superficiality and desire significance and their answer will be yes.

Jesus certainly intended the church to offer these things—authentic connection, belonging, significance. Yet it's clear he also intended the church to separate and to confront. Then, as now, the followers of Jesus are called to be "set apart," to be substantively, demonstrably different and thereby transformative (like salt and light), to "carry your cross," to "go and make disciples, teaching them to obey," to be in the world but not of the world. These very actions, in Jesus' own words, are adults say growing closer to or learning about God are the two most important reasons to attend church. And with all the other options open to Millennials, it's safe to conclude that, when they show up at church for a worship or learning opportunity, they do so hoping there is Someone present to worship or learn about.

Do people encounter Jesus in your community of faith? Do your ministries bring people closer to him? Is there a sense, when you gather, that the Spirit is alive among you?

If, at the end of the day, teens and adults can say they met with God in our faith communities, getting them to come back won't be much of an issue. But they won't be coming back for us; they'll be coming back for him.

And that's just as it should be.

Ministry, after all, comes from the Latin root *minus*—"less." As ministers of the gospel of Christ, it should always be less about us and more about him.

often perceived as arrogant, judgmental or, at best, presumptuous. But Jesus commissioned the church to counter culture, to collide rather than collude. The collision reveals our loyalties.

Millennials call for "genuine community," and the church should certainly be a genuine community. Yet Millennials also seem to want the church to be inclusive, non-judgmental and tolerant. Seldom do we hear calls for holiness (set-apart-ness) or righteousness, despite the abundant emphasis on those attributes in scripture.

The central question is not what the next generation wants, but what Jesus wants.

To see the next generation flourish in their faith, we should focus less on engineering an experience or program for them and more on being who Jesus called us to be. The authenticity of our own discipleship may be precisely the example younger Christians, and non-believers, hope to see in us.

How might this look? Compassion's philosophy of child and youth development can be distilled to three simple things: *known*, *loved* and *protected*. Regardless of culture, children and young people are more likely to thrive when at least one, non-relative adult knows, engages with and encourages them, as they do in Compassion's programs. To be loved includes being listened to and valued; therefore, youth voice and participation in their own faith-building experiences is important. Children around the world, including in the U.S., face risks of trauma. Protection from traumatic events, such as child abuse, sex trafficking or bullying, should be a priority for churches that genuinely live out the love of Jesus.

The best thing we can do to encourage faith in the next generation is to be examples of genuine faith that is worthy of imitation. Regardless of cultural context, our efforts should focus on becoming the church Jesus intended us to be.

LEADERSHIP 3

Are Millennials fundamentally a narcissistic generation? Or the next-greatest generation? A generation of entrepreneurs? Or a generation of couch surfers? Or maybe a bit of all of the above?

As you seek to lead and mentor Millennials, the way you answer these questions—the way you label and define the young adults you work with—will impact your success.

Some see kids who need discipline and a good old-fashioned work ethic.

Others see a generation of potential leaders, motivated by grand visions and hungry to live lives that matter, that make an indelible mark for the better on the world.

The established leader who can see this potential in Millennials, and who is willing to meet them in their desire for meaning, will find an engaged and eager group ready to channel their innate resources—their desire to create not just consume, their technological savvy, their entrepreneurial spirit—toward the mission of God's kingdom.

What does it look like for this kind of visionary, hopeful leader to effectively engage Millennials? Out of Barna's research—as well as in much of the research from the secular marketplace—there are four factors that emerge as essential to developing the next generation of spiritual leaders: authenticity, significance, reverse mentoring and vocational discipleship.

AUTHENTICITY

It's a word that gets bandied about a lot in connection with Millennials—and, indeed, it's a word Millennials are themselves particularly fond of. But what does it mean exactly? What does it look like to "be authentic"?

It means being true to who you are. Don't represent yourself as something you're not. This goes for individuals and for institutions. Since the moment they were plunked down in front of the TV to watch Saturday

> Young adults are looking for leaders willing to admit they're not perfect.

morning cartoons, Millennials have been relentlessly marketed to. As easy as breathing, most can spot the "catch"—the message behind the message. They know when you're trying to sell something.

But their skepticism is about something deeper than advertising. While savvy to the tricks of marketing, most Millennials see it as an understandable business necessity. They admire ad man Don Draper of AMC's drama *Mad Men*. In fact, good marketing is a type of creative genius Millennials can respect, even as they try themselves to be "above it." Businesses are trying to sell them something and they get that. What they don't accept—and what they've seen far too much of—is corruption among people and institutions purporting to do good.

Many of the institutions previous generations respected as pillars of a healthy society have been disgraced by scandals during Millennials' formative years. Corruption has been exposed within trusted institutions like government, big corporations, national sports teams and organized religion. From President Clinton to Lance Armstrong, from Tiger Woods to the Catholic church, from the NSA to Martha Stewart, Millennials have plenty of reasons to be skeptical.

In *You Lost Me*, Barna president David Kinnaman calls this kind of skepticism "institutional doubt," and for many young adults it leads to disconnection from church and even faith. Fully one-fifth of Catholic Millennials say "the priest-abuse scandals have made me question my faith." Nearly one out of eight young Christians (13%) say they "used to work at a church and became disillusioned." (This number includes both church staff and volunteers.) Think about it: Tens of thousands of twentysomethings have been hurt and disappointed while trying to serve the church—sometimes so badly they've walked away from their community of faith.

Christian institutions that call themselves good—that say they're dedicated to the redemption and restoration of human beings—have too often shown themselves to be as damaging and profit-seeking as deceitful oil companies, unscrupulous hedge-fund managers and dishonest politicians. How can Christian leaders begin to repair the damage?

Young adults aren't looking for perfect leaders. They are looking for leaders willing to admit they're not perfect. Hypocrisy is one of the biggest criticisms Millennials have of Christians. A full two-thirds of Millennials believe American churchgoers are a lot or somewhat hypocritical.

As you lead and mentor twentysomethings, seek to embody the value of authenticity. Don't try to be "cool"—to wear what they wear or hang out where they hang out (unless you already do). Don't pretend you're perfect or that you have it all figured out.

Instead, lead from your strengths and be honest about your weaknesses. Neither false humility nor insincere bravado will win you friends among young adults. As Millennials come of age and face some of the tougher stuff of life—economic instability, unemployment, breakups, illnesses, difficult relationships and so on—they are looking for leaders who model what it looks like to respond to God in the midst of turbulence.

SIGNIFICANCE

In his Barna FRAME, *20 and Something*, author David H. Kim tells the story of a twentysomething he mentored. Stephanie, a recent college graduate, was offered a coveted job opportunity at Google, which she ultimately turned down to work instead at a small nonprofit for barely more than minimum wage. For many, the mere idea of turning down job security, a great salary and the opportunity to work for an industry-leading company with a world-changing mission would be incomprehensible. But after weeks of careful deliberation, Stephanie did just that. Despite her parents' best efforts to convince her otherwise, she stuck to her convictions and spent the next few years serving this small nonprofit with whose mission she felt a strong connection.

Stephanie's decision reflects a significant trend among Millennials: They want to make an impact. Barna research for *20 and Something* shows that Millennials want passion for their job (42%) even more than a job that helps them become financially secure (34%) or that provides enough money to enjoy life (24%). And according to a 2012 Net Impact Study, graduating university students say they would go so far as to take a 15% pay cut for a job that makes a social or environmental impact (45%) or to work for an organization with similar values to their own (58%). In the same survey, 72% of those students said having a job where they can make an impact is essential to their happiness—compared to 53% of all Americans.

And if they don't find it? They'll leave. Nine in 10 Millennials expect to stay in a job only about three years.

PASTORS, YOUTH WORKERS & MENTORS

• What do you really think about Millennials—and how does your perception color your expectations of and impact your work with teens and young adults?

• How honest are you about your own struggles—and what can you do to more intentionally model authenticity?

• Are you teachable—and how can you be more humble and open to mutuality in mentoring Millennials?

David H. Kim serves as the executive director of the Center for Faith & Work (CFW) at Redeemer Presbyterian Church in New York City and as Pastor of Faith and Work at Redeemer. Prior to joining CFW in 2007, David served as a chaplain at Princeton University, where he also served as the founder and executive director of Manna Christian Fellowship. He has written two devotional books that connect the narrative of Scripture to our lives today: Glimpses of a Greater Glory: A Devotional through the Storyline of the Bible *and* The Lord's Prayer Devotional. *He's also the author of* 20 and Something: Have the Time of Your Life (and Figure it All Out Too).

What are some of the misperceptions about Millennials that drive people to underestimate them? How can those who are leading Millennials look beyond those stereotypes and embrace the more positive attributes of Millennials?

Millennials are often viewed as not willing to do the grunt work associated with many entry-level jobs. And it's true that menial work is often eschewed by Millennials, and their motivation tends to diminish very quickly. Previous generations understood this mundaneness as the accepted way to advance in most careers: You pay your dues and, decades later, you get to do work that's more meaningful. This leads older generations to assume Millennials' disdain of mundaneness comes from a misguided sense of entitlement and a naiveté about how life "really" works.

While it may very well be true that Millennials don't prefer menial and mundane work—who does?—this generation has, in their lifetime, seen the flattening and democratization of many industries. They've seen that you don't have to wait until you're 50-plus to make your millions, or to become a CEO, or to create a product or service that revolutionizes an industry. Their peers have done it already. Why waste time carrying boxes when you can reinvent the box? Most understand that not everybody will accomplish such lofty goals, but they have unprecedented potential to accomplish their dreams. This is their new norm.

Millennials have a strong desire to change their environments, and anyone leading them needs to give them space, literally and figuratively, to make a visible impact. It takes a lot of humility from older generations, but I find that when you give Millennials space to dream, they not only do the grunt work but they own it—because they are meaningfully participating in creating larger possibilities. Grunt work for the promise of meaningful work in the future will not motivate Millennials. But tapping into their desire to change some part of their world will bring out a host of gifts and talents that might otherwise go to waste.

Why is it so important to connect with long-term vision and meaningful impact when leading Millennials? Practically, what does that look like? How do you connect your vision as an organization with the dreams and personal passions of Millennials?

Working with Millennials, I find it helpful to take a monthly offsite to communicate, assess and realign the "big-picture" of whatever we're doing.

Communicating the big picture inspires ownership in the group because they see the whys behind all their work, which can get easily lost in the day-to-day grind. They see how their routine tasks connect to the big picture, and this brings a sense of connectivity and collaboration.

Assessing gives Millennials a voice and an opportunity to critique the big picture and the hows of accomplishing it. Assessment inspires group ownership, but it also reveals to everyone the passions, gifts and blind spots of the individuals on the team. This is important for identifying future leadership potential or if someone is a poor fit in their current position.

Realignment to the big picture allows the team to evaluate if their day-to-day is accomplishing the overall goal. The end result should be clear, actionable steps toward accomplishing the goal. Allowing Millennials to come up with these actionable steps encourages them to own their tasks and connects them to the organization's mission.

What are the four most important things to keep in mind as a leader or mentor of Millennials?

- Give lots of feedback, reinforcing—in real-time, if possible—what they've done well and what could be better.

- Be authentic and wisely transparent; they respect it, and they can tell very quickly when someone is being insincere.

- Try not to exert your position or authority to motivate or lead Millennials. They don't respect authority for authority's sake, because they've experienced many reasons to distrust authority figures. Offer the reasons behind your requests and be willing to hear their perspective.

- Be willing to admit your own faults and blind spots, and be open to how you can improve.

I'M LOOKING FOR A JOB THAT...[1]

42% ...I FEEL PASSIONATE ABOUT

34% ...OFFERS ME FINANCIAL SECURITY

24% ...GIVES ME ENOUGH MONEY TO ENJOY LIFE

HAVING A JOB WHERE I CAN MAKE AN IMPACT IS ESSENTIAL TO MY HAPPINESS [2]

ALL AMERICANS — 53%

72% — GRADUATING UNIVERSITY STUDENTS

I EXPECT TO MAKE AN IMPACT THROUGH WORK [3] (AMONG GRADUATING UNIVERSITY STUDENTS)

YES, WITHIN 5 YEARS	37%
YES, IN 6+ YEARS	28%
DON'T KNOW / NO ANSWER	23%
NO	12%

ALL OTHER THINGS BEING EQUAL, I'D TAKE A 15% PAYCUT... [4] (AMONG GRADUATING UNIVERSITY STUDENTS)

45% ...FOR A JOB THAT MAKES A SOCIAL OR ENVIRONMENTAL IMPACT

58% ...TO WORK FOR AN ORGANIZATION WITH VALUES LIKE MY OWN

[1] Barna FRAMES, 20 and Something by David H. Kim; [2] 2012 Net Impact study, "What Workers Want"; [3] Ibid; [4] Ibid

In order to work (or minister) effectively with Millennials, it's critical not to underestimate how important significance is to them. As a generation, they have an undeserved reputation for a lack of loyalty. As a rule, however, this is inaccurate. While it's true that Millennials do not generally demonstrate loyalty to *organizations* or *institutions*, most are extremely loyal to *causes* and *people*.

What does this mean for you and the Millennials you lead? The good news is, young adults want a meaningful cause—and what's more meaningful than the cause of Christ? The difficulty comes in connecting that cause with the "trivialities" and tasks of daily work and ministry.

Our research shows that few churches help young people discover a sense of mission, though doing so is important in cultivating a faith that lasts. Millennials who remain active in church are twice as likely as dropouts to say they served the poor through their church (33% versus 14%). They are also more likely to say they went on a trip that helped expand their thinking (29% versus 16%) and more likely to indicate they had found a cause or issue at church that motivates them (25% versus 10%). (See Figure 3.4 for more on this dynamic.)

Churches that establish a direct link between their mission and the tasks involved in achieving it are more able to build and maintain a leadership core of young adults. Plus, Millennials often learn about what they are working on—the "why" behind the "what" and "how." So as they assume leadership roles, young leaders will also work to make the connection for others between practicalities and significance.

BUSINESS & NONPROFIT LEADERS

• When you think about employing or working with Millennials, what assumptions about them do you bring to the table—and how do those perceptions influence your posture toward young adults?

• Do the Millennials in your organization know what part they play in accomplishing the mission—and how can you better communicate the significance of their contribution?

• Do you see the people in your organization as disciples following Jesus in their career, their vocation—and what could you do to emphasize and enhance this understanding among employees and/or volunteers?

A third thing Barna has learned about effective leadership of Millennials is that young people want to be taken seriously today—not just for some distant future leadership position. In their eyes, institutional church life is too hierarchical. They're not interested in earning their way to the top so much as they want to put their gifts and skills to work for the local church in the present—not future—tense.

This sense of not being taken seriously or of being unable to make an impact creates a real sense of angst among many Millennials. Nearly three in 10 (28%) feel held back at their job because of their age and another 23% say they worry their older co-workers do not respect them because of their age. Their desire to be taken seriously and to be given real responsibility is something churches should take note of—and be eager to fulfill. What better place for young Christian Millennials to feel they can truly make a difference with their gifts and talents than at their churches?

The term "reverse mentoring" has come to describe the give and take between young and established leaders. Effective mentoring of Millennial leaders means helping young believers discover their own mission in the world, not merely asking them to wait their turn.

One way to think about this generation is as exiles in something like a "digital Babylon"—an immersive, interactive, image-rich environment where many older believers feel foreign and lost. More than six in 10 Millennials like that they know more about technology than older adults. And, the truth is, the church needs the next generation's help to navigate digital terrains.

Aside from a fluency in technology, you might look to your Millennials to "mentor" you in the following areas:

- *Global perspective*—Millennials are often well-traveled, culturally pluralistic and knowledgeable about the world.

- *Sustainability ideas*—From the environment to fair trade, Millennials are hyper-aware of consumerism's effects on the world.

- *Social concern*—From founding non-profits to buying TOMS shoes, justice issues are on many Millennials' minds and hearts.

- *Optimism*—Millennials often have a can-do attitude and an expansive expectation of what's possible.

- *Entrepreneurial spirit*—Crowd-sourcing sites like Kickstarter and Indiegogo have helped to cultivate an entrepreneurial culture among young adults around the world; many are unafraid to try things that have never been done before.

> Effective mentoring means helping young believers discover their own mission in the world, not asking them to wait their turn.

Finally, perhaps there is no greater opportunity for mentoring and leading Millennials than through vocational discipleship. As they to find their way in the world, one of their most critical issues of identity is calling. They have spent much of their life up until now preparing for what they would "do"—for a career. That job, whether it's a dream job or not, is where they spend the bulk of their time; seven in 10 (70%) name it as central to their identity.

▶ 3.2 MILLENNIALS' CAREER PRIORITIES ARE...

1 FUNDING MY PERSONAL INTERESTS (29%)

2 WORKING FOR MYSELF (24%)

3 A JOB ADAPTABLE TO MY STRENGTHS (21%)

4 A LOT OF VARIETY (17%)

5 FREEDOM TO TAKE RISKS (9%)

70% MILLENNIALS WHO SAY THEIR CAREER IS CENTRAL TO THEIR IDENTITY

Millennials see their 20s as a time to explore their career options so they can find a job that will provide the necessary sense of meaning and fulfillment. Because job satisfaction and making an impact are so important to them, Millennials refuse to compromise on what they want out of work—which is a lot: They cite working for themselves, a job adaptable to their strengths, having a lot of variety and the freedom to take risks as essential career priorities, in addition to being able to fund their personal interests.

Joseph Cavanaugh III is president of Equip 2 Equip LLC, dedicated to equipping leaders to equip others. He is the author of The Language of Blessing *and has worked as both an entrepreneur and ministry leader in many capacities, including serving as the founding president of the Mobile Electronics Retailers Association, as Executive Director of New Life Ministries and as Leader of Gallup's Global Faith Practice Division. He and his wife, Jaynee, live in Omaha, Nebraska, and have five sons and three grandchildren.*

Our research shows that only about one-third of Christians feel called to their current occupation. Among younger Christians the number is even greater—about 44% feel a disconnect between their perceived calling and their current employment. How can people living in this tension repair this divide?
An overly simple response is that these younger Christians have never been equipped to live out who God has created and called then to be. They often lack integral self-awareness. Fortunately, this can be learned.

The majority of young Christians I work with have no idea who they really are, let alone their gifts or life calling. It is an exhilarating journey as they discover they have been created in Jesus as a unique expression of God's workmanship, and that the Father has prepared good works and a calling for them to walk in.

How would you describe the relationship between self-awareness and success—both in terms of one's career and one's faith?

Research consistently shows that self-awareness is a foundational quality of career success. Leaders who lack self-awareness, on the other hand, are a disaster for themselves and for those they lead.

Self-awareness is equally important when it comes to faith. People who are spiritually self-aware have a non-anxious presence—they are completely at peace with who God has created and called them to be. They are deeply grateful to God for his gifts and calling in their lives while fully realizing these gifts are neither earned nor deserved, but given freely for the benefit of others.

Learning how to be self-aware starts with recognizing what I call the "cycle of false identity." This cycle begins in a family where the parents are not very self-aware, and they place unfounded expectations on their children. When the children fail to meet those unfounded expectations, the parents judge them in their failure.

The more we try to meet our parents' unfounded expectations, the more we begin to lose our authentic sense of self. We begin to feel like we are somehow defective—we are not good enough, smart enough, hardworking enough. Our whole sense of identity becomes distorted.

The process of breaking the cycle of false identity is an equipping process. The Greek word for equipping means to restore, to complete, to perfect. Restoring a person back to God's original design is a critical part of breaking the cycle. We want to create a cycle of authentic identity. We can help people become self-aware by helping them rediscover their gifts and talents. As they receive those gifts and talents with a grateful heart, it produces true humility, which produces authenticity. From authenticity, love and service arise—and their light begins to shine.

How can we discern between a Western, individualistic sense of calling and a biblical understanding of calling?
Western individualism is primarily focused on fulfilling wants and desires. Biblical individualism is about what we have been given for the benefit of others. It is about fulfilling our unique function, contribution and calling.

King David beautifully articulates in many of his psalms how intimate God's love is for each of us as individuals. Centuries later, in his letters to the Corinthians and to the Romans, Paul emphasizes the great diversity of gifts and functions that exist in the Body of Christ. He also points out that each individual's contribution is indispensable and vital for the benefit of the whole Body. A final reality communicated in the parable of the talents and again in the book of Revelation is that each of us will stand before the Lord and give an account of what we did with what we were so generously given—and that will be an individual experience.

We are each created individually to be interdependent with one another. We are designed by God to serve each other with all that we have been uniquely gifted through grace.

Given how much time and energy Millennials spend at work and the pressure they put on that work to be fulfilling, it's not surprising that work is also an area of acute anxiety for many of them. Meaning, purpose, fulfillment and change-the-world impact? That's a lot of pressure to put on a job. Perhaps that's why nealry half of young adults (49%) feel anxious about choosing their career for fear they'll make the wrong choice. And maybe why Millennials rank their career as their number-one area for improvement; only about one in five (19%) say they are extremely satisfied with their career. For many Christian Millennials, this anxiety is compounded by a desire to know and follow God's will for their life—which includes their career. That's why it's particularly alarming to know that only one-third of Christian young adults feel called to their work. Nearly half (48%) think God is calling them to different work, but haven't yet been willing to make the change.

▶ 3.3 FEELING UNEASY

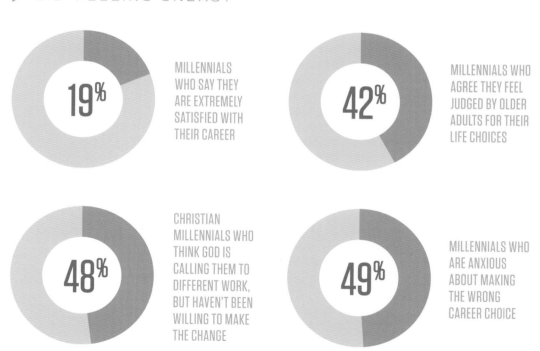

19% MILLENNIALS WHO SAY THEY ARE EXTREMELY SATISFIED WITH THEIR CAREER

42% MILLENNIALS WHO AGREE THEY FEEL JUDGED BY OLDER ADULTS FOR THEIR LIFE CHOICES

48% CHRISTIAN MILLENNIALS WHO THINK GOD IS CALLING THEM TO DIFFERENT WORK, BUT HAVEN'T BEEN WILLING TO MAKE THE CHANGE

49% MILLENNIALS WHO ARE ANXIOUS ABOUT MAKING THE WRONG CAREER CHOICE

This is where vocational discipleship comes in. Because Millennials are so concerned about the significance of what they do, older Christians who are also established professionals or tradespeople can help them 1) identify their life's work, and 2) help them connect it to their identity as a Christian. There is no sense of compartmentalization with Millennials—they expect their Christianity, their profession and their relationships to be integrated. The church is in a unique position to help them accomplish this in a way no other organization can.

However, most Millennials—really, most adults in general—do not experience this kind of guidance from their community of faith. More than one-third of Christian Millennials (37%) do not have an older mentor who gives them advice about work. Almost two-thirds of all churched adults (63%) say that, in the past three years, they have not received any teachings or information that helped shape or challenge their views on work and career.

The church has a rich tradition of helping people understand how vocation fits within God's greater work in the world. Millennials' desire to see their work make a difference demands a revived focus on those teachings in order to help them practice a more holistic understanding of identity and calling.

Among many Millennials who grew up in church and who are still in church today, vocational discipleship has played a key role in their formative church experiences. Millennials who remain active in church are more than twice as likely as dropouts to have learned how Christians can positively contribute to society (46% vs. 20%) and nearly four times more likely to say they better understand their purpose in life through church (45% vs. 12%). Additionally, those who are still active are three times more likely than dropouts to say they learned to view their gifts and passions as part of God's calling (45% vs. 17%). They are four times more likely to have learned at church "how the Bible applies to my field or career interests" (29% vs. 7%). A similar gap exists when it comes to having received helpful input from a pastor about education (21% vs. 5%). Helping young adults connect the dots between faith and work makes a difference to their lifelong pursuit of Jesus.

The church has a rich tradition of helping people understand how vocation fits within God's greater work in the world.

What makes ministry to Millennials effective? Young adults who remain active in local churches after high school have substantially different experiences compared with young adults who leave the church. They tend to have a wider range of positive life inputs during their high school years—particularly when it comes to how faith relates to vocation, cultural discernment and life decisions. Although survey research does not prove causation, these findings suggest that multi-faceted efforts with Millennials may help to facilitate a more lasting faith.

● ACTIVE
● DROPOUT

% AMONG 18-29 YEAR OLDS WITH A PROTESTANT BACKGROUND

HAD A CLOSE PERSONAL FRIEND WHO WAS AN ADULT AT CHURCH OR PARISH

59%   31%

HAD AN ADULT MENTOR AT CHURCH, OTHER THAN THE PASTOR OR CHURCH STAFF

28%   11%

LEARNED ABOUT HOW CHRISTIANS CAN POSITIVELY CONTRIBUTE TO SOCIETY

46%   20%

BETTER UNDERSTAND MY PURPOSE IN LIFE THROUGH CHURCH

45%   12%

LEARNED TO VIEW MY GIFTS AND PASSIONS AS PART OF GOD'S CALLING

45%   17%

LEARNED HOW THE BIBLE APPLIES TO MY FIELD OR CAREER INTERESTS

29%   7%

SERVED THE POOR THROUGH MY CHURCH

33%   14%

WENT ON A TRIP THAT HELPED ME EXPAND MY THINKING

29%   16%

FOUND A CAUSE OR ISSUE AT CHURCH THAT MOTIVATED ME

25%   10%

RECEIVED HELPFUL INPUT FROM A PASTOR OR CHURCH WORKER ABOUT MY EDUCATION

21%   5%

RECEIVED A SCHOLARSHIP FOR COLLEGE THROUGH CHURCH

5%   2%

In leading young adults, what did you find are the key factors to effectively engage them?

Young adults want to have a connection to something larger than themselves so that, regardless of the level they're working at, they can gauge their impact on a significant social issue. I've also found that young people want to be engaged and contribute meaningfully to discussions and problem solving. To assume that fewer years of work experience means they don't have insight on complex problems leaves them feeling uninspired. Providing the opportunity to develop their professional skills also helps to keep Millennials engaged.

What did you find most inspiring about the young adults you worked with at Teach for America?

Teach For America does a phenomenal job attracting motivated, passionate young adults to their very important mission. Everyone I worked with at Teach For America had a deep commitment to tackle educational inequity in our nation's public schools. They were willing to do whatever it took to help their low-income students achieve. And it was infectious!

Beyond their commitment, my young colleagues were incredibly intelligent, goal-oriented and optimistic—a fabulous combination that will ensure young adults have a lasting, positive impact on urban and rural public education.

Why do you think it's so important for young adults to connect their work to a greater cause?

Most of us long to make a difference in the world. As much as that idea is something of a cliché, it does ring true. We want to find purpose and meaning in our daily lives. And for young adults who are growing up in an increasingly complex world, making meaning becomes even more important. The world's problems—global warming, income inequality, terrorism, hunger and limited education opportunities for the poor (just to name a few!)—are daunting. When young adults connect their work to one of these social problems, they contribute to solving the greatest issues our society faces. There is something inspiring and rewarding about work that goes beyond your small corner, or cubicle, of the world.

Nicole Baker Fulgham is the founder and president of The Expectations Project, a nonprofit organization that develops and mobilizes faith-motivated advocates to close the academic achievement gap in public schools. She is the author of Educating All God's Children: What Christians Can—and Should—Do to Improve Public Education for Low-Income Kids *and the Barna FRAME* Schools in Crisis: They Need Your Help (Whether You Have Kids or Not).

• If you had to define
your real, deep-down
view of Millennials,
what would you say—
and how do you think
this perception affects
your ability to teach or
train them?

• What are some
ways you can help
Millennials connect
learning and service,
so they understand
the significance of the
knowledge they're
gaining?

• How are you
helping young
adults connect what
they're learning with
obedience to God's
call on their lives—and
how could you nurture
in them a robust,
thoroughly Christian
understanding of
vocation?

What might vocational discipleship look like in your organization, practically speaking? Here are a few ideas:

- Identify Christian professionals or tradespersons who can commit to in-depth relationships (mentoring, but with a vocational focus), or even just provide exposure (such as a ride-along with a Christian police officer, or any other profession where a young person could spend a day with a Christian at his or her secular workplace).

- Provide explicit training for how to live out Christianity in the workplace—seminars, case studies, personal stories.

- Offer assessments and counseling for those who are selecting a trade, a college or a degree path.

- Offer vocational counseling for those struggling to find work or making an unplanned work transition.

- Provide workspaces and other specialized facilities for those who need a place to work, network or develop a new idea; consider staffing it with retired church members who can lend advice or a listening ear.

- Offer apprenticeships and internships—formal or informal—with businesses that have a focus on values.

- Offer community service opportunities or missions trips in which Millennials work side by side with people using secular skills in a ministry context (e.g., medical or aviation missionaries, skilled labor, pro-bono lawyers, etc.)

WORKING & LEADING TOGETHER

In the not-too-distant past, the most common method of career training was apprenticeship. An unskilled worker who showed promise was apprenticed to a master craftsperson, training under his or her guidance until the apprentice could carry out first the basic and, eventually, the highly skilled aspects of the craft. Even from the very beginning, although she didn't yet have the knowledge or skill to work on her own, the apprentice was right in the thick of it, in the shop alongside the master and other apprentices of varying skill levels, learning the rhythms of the craft and offering her brute strength and boundless enthusiasm to the shop's success.

There is much to recommend this kind of training, especially when it comes to training leaders. But whether out of a selfish desire not to be inconvenienced or, worse, a competitive impulse to guard our turf, we often shoo young potential leaders out of the workshop—or, if they're lucky, sit them down on a bench to watch us work.

What a waste.

Yes, Millennials' boundless energy is sometimes too much for the nuance demanded by the craft. Sure, their enthusiasm can occasionally overwhelm common sense.

But Jesus didn't write Peter off for lack of nuance and a deficit of common sense. No, he saw that Peter's strength would sustain the fledgling Jesus community through years of persecution and suffering. He saw that Peter's enthusiasm would take him beyond the circle of Jewish Jesus-followers to welcome Gentiles into God's family.

May God grant us similar vision as we train the next generation of leaders for the church.

 ▶ Q & A W I T H K U R T W I L L E M S *

In your experience, what is the biggest hurdle to life-giving mentoring relationships that nurture young leaders?

Too often mentorship becomes something like mold-er-ship: Trying to create clones who create more clones. Millennial leaders long to become more fully human—more of who we are meant to be—not merely a younger version of our mentor. What those of us in our 20s and early 30s crave more than anything from spiritual and ministry mentors is safety. In many mentoring situations that go bad, the number-one complicating factor comes down to a mentor who is uncomfortable creating safe space for their mentee to ask questions, to doubt or even to disagree.

The church's crisis of mentoring is that leaders with a few more years of experience under their belt fail to create safe space for younger leaders. As the foundational posture of mentoring, safety yields life-changing influence.

What do you see as the essential postures of a mentor?

Safety—the ability to create spaces where no questions or perspectives are off limits. Many of us (I'm on the older end of the Millennial spectrum) yearn for seasoned saints who make asking questions and wrestling with difficult issues normative in our conversations about God and life. Millennials want the freedom to create a future for the church that may look different from our parents' experience. But that future doesn't have to be discontinuous from the past. Safety yields influence—and rarely will a Millennial follower of Jesus disregard our previous experiences. Many of us are quicker to integrate our roots into who we are becoming than to abandon them altogether. Safety within mentoring relationships gives us the freedom to hold tradition and innovation together.

Authentic modeling—showing mentees through their patterns of living that mentors walk what they talk. The

Kurt Willems is founding pastor of Pangea Communities, a church plant located in Seattle. He is a graduate student focusing on early Christianity, Greco-Roman Religions and Classical Languages, and he writes from a missional Anabaptist perspective for various publications. Find Kurt on Twitter @KurtWillems and Facebook.com/ KurtWillems, and at KurtWillems.com. His first book is forthcoming.

best mentors I've had pattern their lifestyles consistent with their spoken values. They don't simply encourage a solid work ethic, for instance, but they show it. These mentors have a deep passion for living out the way of Jesus in everyday life, not out of obligation but out of joy.

Life-long discovery—mentors who adapt, grow, change and learn throughout their journey. Forrest was my boss during my college internship in a church youth ministry. One thing he instilled in me during those formative years is "leaders are learners." What did we do together? We read books! The very thing that had been a chore during high school became a growth engine that would lead me into greater effectiveness as a future pastor. And although reading still isn't a natural way for me to pass the time, books have become foundational in my ongoing theological and pastoral development. Through mentors like Forrest I've become convinced that life-long learning and discovery is essential for discipleship. He modeled this sort of commitment and made it contagious.

Mutuality—seeing mentoring as two-directional. Mentoring relationships of this sort energize Millennials. We don't want to feel as though we have nothing to contribute. If the relationship isn't a two-way street, we start to wonder if we are simply a means to building the ego of our so-called mentor. We younger folks have things to teach older generations. Admittedly, we aren't always good at articulating our ideas with tact or grace—which leads to the next essential posture of Millennial mentoring:

Patience—a commitment to walk with a mentee for the long haul. Transformation should be more like a journey and less like an agenda item. One person who tried to play a mentoring role in my life implemented what he called "power meetings." We had 10 minutes to hash out issues, so as not to disrupt his busy day. When it comes to mentoring, "power meetings" are like wearing socks with flip-flops. They just don't go together. Mentoring is a relational commitment that involves one of life's most precious commodities: time. We need mentors who are committed to our growth for the long haul, and who are patient enough to stick with us when we make poor choices along the way.

Intentionality—mentors who think through ways to help mentees grow into the most human versions of themselves. Mentoring, though not mechanical, ought to have some level of intention. What themes or ideas will be discussed regularly: spiritual journey, theology, sports, family, ministry, hobbies? How will these conversations lead to potential growth? What are some next steps that may be helpful for the mentee? These are some questions that might be helpful in guiding discussion times together.

What are five things Millennials want to hear from a mentor?
"I want to journey with you for the long haul because I believe in you." Millennials yearn for affirmation from seasoned saints. When Jesus called young fishermen to follow him, he was letting them know he believed in them, even as he invited them to believe in

him. Jesus saw the potential of Peter and the other disciples and drew it out in such a way that they inaugurated a world-changing movement. Imagine the possibilities when mentors, filled with the Spirit of Christ, believe in the potential of Millennials. It could change our world!

"Don't limit yourself to what seems realistic, but expect to discover new possibilities." Twenty- and 30-somethings do not lack for imagination. We actually believe God can use us to do great things for the Kingdom. We need mentors who recognize the possibilities, not just the rationalities, who understand life with God as a creative process and who see our potential and guide it in a constructive direction. When we fail, we need encouragement. When we succeed, we need someone to celebrate with us. When we can't see the way forward, we need someone to help us discern.

"Let's come up with a mentoring rhythm tailored to your passions and gifts." Rather than having an agenda, this approach takes into account the whole person. Sometimes this will mean more than conversations over coffee or dinner. It might include the mentor and mentee serving together with their hands and feet. As the mentor customizes the process to the individual he or she is discipling, the mentee will mature in their innate abilities and grow in their God-given identity.

"Nothing is off limits. We can talk about anything with an open mind." Safety again. Whether talking about struggles, theology, politics, sex or any other heated conversation point, a mentor who is willing to hold his or her viewpoints with open hands will create space for mutual transformation. Again, each person involved has something to teach the other. Millennials want to know we are not going to be rejected or disregarded just because we have a perspective that is different from the mentor.

"I can't wait to grow and learn with you! We have so much to learn from each other." Millennials want to journey with someone, not trail behind a supposed mentor who thinks they have already arrived. We also want to know our mentors plan to stick around for the long haul, not for a short season. The dynamics of this friendship may change over time, but a commitment to grow will move both parties forward into new experiences in life and ministry.

* Adapted from the Spring/Summer 2014 (Vol. 12.1) issue of *Conversations: A Forum for Authentic Transformation* and from Kurt's Patheos.com blog. Used by permission.

What is your favorite place to connect with God? To connect with others? How about the best place to spend time in personal reflection?

To some extent, every church facility is an effort to harmonize these and other competing demands. The buildings where communities of faith gather are expected to do triple duty (at least) as spaces for worship and prayer, friendship and mentoring, and spiritual self-discovery. But if you're like many people, the place you feel closest to God is different from the place you enjoy spending time with friends—and both may be different from the place you go to be alone with your thoughts. To complicate matters, different people have differing ideas about the right "feel" for a place to connect with God . . . to say nothing of their divergent opinions about where best to interface with others or turn inward in meditation.

It's trendy in some circles to decry the importance of space. Why spend any more resources than absolutely necessary on walls, windows and carpet? What's really needed is a functional area that houses worship, teaching and fellowship. Anything more than utilitarian is irrelevant at best and wasteful at worst—maybe even sacrilegious.

But such an attitude ignores human experience. Are we not intent on developing spaces for our own comfort? When hosting others in our homes, do we not clean, straighten and rearrange, so as to give them the most inviting and comfortable experience possible? In our work lives we acknowledge the necessity of space that is both functional (to be productive) and comfortable (to be creative). If such efforts are good enough for us and for our social guests, are they not also good enough for God and our spiritual guests?

Any visit to Europe would be incomplete without a visit to a few of the spectacular cathedrals. For anyone born and raised on this side of the Atlantic, the scope of time those churches represent can be dizzying. "Let's take a look at the new pipe organ," the tour guide might say, before showing you

To some extent, every church facility is an effort to harmonize competing demands.

an instrument installed 150 years ago. It's "new" because the old organ was made 400 years ago. The structures themselves were often constructed over the course of several generations or even centuries. What made our spiritual forefathers invest so much time, talent, and treasure into these buildings? Why doesn't such an investment in church facilities seem appropriate today? Has our culture lost its respect for the physical trappings of a sacred space, or do we just have different trappings (pipe organ out; $25,000 projector in)?

In *The Hunchback of Notre Dame*, Victor Hugo waxes eloquent on the decline of cathedrals and of their impact on Christianity. Claude Frollo, the archdeacon of the cathedral, points to a book, then to Notre Dame and predicts, "This will replace that." As new printing technologies made the written word more accessible, books would supplant churches as the primary means by which everyday people encountered God.

His prediction came true. Cathedrals were built not only to house teaching and worship, but to proclaim the gospel and convey doctrine, theology and Scripture. Now we use other technological means to do the same. In Hugo's day, the primary means was the book. Today it's the blog, the podcast, Twitter and Instagram.

With the advent of new ways to communicate the gospel, we can afford to expect much less of our buildings.

It is unlikely that any generation—let alone Millennials, who are so at home in the digital space—will seek to recreate the physical spaces of the past. But the question is worth asking: What are we losing along the way? As we develop religious spaces fit for the twenty-first century, how can we also maintain the timeless principles of sacred space that have been developed through centuries of architecture and design?

The old churches were built to connect people to God. The altar, the stained glass windows, the soaring ceiling that pointed to the heavens—every element was designed to create a link between human and divine.

Generally speaking, modern churches are *not* designed with this goal in mind. In fact, many modern churches are explicitly constructed not to look and feel too much like a religious place. A modern church is designed to host activities, and these activities point the people to God. But strip away those activities and you might as well be at a community college or a performing arts center or, heaven help us, an airport terminal.

Most of our modern churches have excellent areas set aside for corporate worship, group learning and community-building. But they leave something to be desired when it comes to personal reflection and prayer.

How do these changes impact Millennials? They may or may not be the next "greatest generation," but they are certainly the next largest. With about 78 million of them in the US, they are an important demographic for any organization to understand, and churches are no exception.

To understand the principles of design that best resonate with Millennials,

Barna Group partnered with CKN to conduct a multi-phase research program. First, we recruited Millennials from a variety of religious backgrounds to tour through urban cathedrals, suburban megachurches, city parks and coffee shops. Along the way we asked them what they liked and didn't like about each space, what they would use different spaces for, and how they might change them if given the opportunity.

Once we had observed Millennials in the field, we better understood the scope of issues confronting churches as they work to optimize their buildings for the next generation. We then developed an online survey and gave it to a nationally representative sample of 18- to 29-year-olds. The combination of in-depth interaction and observation, along with the precision of a large-sample survey, drew into stark relief the key characteristics today's churches must develop if they want to create a sacred environment that meets the needs of Millennials. (For a detailed description of the research, see the Appendices.)

Of course, every person is unique and has her own particular preferences. But there are commonalities—both culturally and within generational cohorts—and knowing these can help leaders make informed decisions about the design of their facilities.

DESCRIPTIONS OF CHURCH

When we asked Millennials to choose words to describe their vision of the ideal church, a two-thirds majority or greater picked the words on the left:

COMMUNITY (78%)   PRIVACY (22%)
SANCTUARY (77%)   AUDITORIUM (23%)
CLASSIC (67%)   TRENDY (33%)
QUIET (65%)   LOUD (35%)
CASUAL (64%)   DIGNIFIED (36%)

- Does your gathering space offer clear visual cues—and what additional visual elements could help Millennials answer the questions "Where am I?" and "What's expected of me?"

- Where do people in your community go for respite—and what could your church do to offer space and atmosphere for peaceful reflection?

- How well do your indoor and outdoor spaces facilitate cultural discernment, reverse mentoring, vocational discipleship, life-shaping relationships and experiences of God—and what could change to make space for Millennials in these areas?

67%

CLASSIC

33%

TRENDY

77%

SANCTUARY

23%

AUDITORIUM

64%

CASUAL

36%

DIGNIFIED

78%

COMMUNITY

22%

PRIVACY

60%

MODERN

40%

TRADITIONAL

56%

PERFORMANCE

44%

RITUAL

67%
QUIET

33%
LOUD

77%
VARIETY

23%
CONSISTENCY

64%
FLEXIBLE

36%
AUTHENTIC

78%
UPBEAT

22%
LOW-KEY

60%
RELAXED

40%
EXCITING

You may associate the words "sanctuary," "classic" and "quiet" with more traditional church buildings—yet less than half of survey respondents preferred the word "traditional" over "modern." (See Figure 4.1.) And herein lies a cognitive dissonance common to survey participants. Many of them seem to aspire to a more traditional church experience, in a beautiful building steeped in history and religious symbolism, but they are more at ease in a modern space that feels more familiar than mysterious.

Our field groups each visited a modern church facility (Willow Creek Community Church in Chicago and Buckhead Church in Atlanta) and a cathedral-style church (St. James Cathedral in Chicago and Church of the Redeemer in Atlanta), and we discovered a similar dissonance among the field participants as in the survey results. At Church of the Redeemer, for example, group members appreciated the Christian symbols grandly displayed in the sanctuary, as well as the magnificent stained glass windows, sweeping arches and soaring ceilings. They felt it was an appropriate space for serious activities such as prayer, coping with tragedy and communing with God, and sensed the spirituality of the place was deep-rooted. At the same time, however, they were concerned about how they would fit in—*If I visit for a service, do I need to wear dressy clothes?*—and a few participants, especially unchurched people, felt overwhelmed or even intimidated by the spiritual intensity of the space.

The same group visited Buckhead Church, and found inviting common areas to connect with others (armchair seating along the edges of an open lobby) and to spend time in personal reflection (smaller private rooms furnished with comfy couches). However, there was no obvious place conducive to connecting with God. One group member suggested that worshiping among a crowd of people in the auditorium might provide that connection, but void of those activities, there was nothing about the facility itself to make a person feel that connection with God. Overall, the "un-churchy" atmosphere of the space, which had more of a corporate vibe than a holy feeling, and the absence of Christian symbols failed to suggest transcendence.

Two metaphors may help to capture the complex relationship between young adults and worship spaces. First, cathedral-style churches seem to Millennials like fine china compared to the everyday dishware of Buckhead and Willow Creek. Fine china is considered higher quality and therefore desirable for special occasions—but it's not appropriate for Tuesday night takeout. We can also see this instinct in nearly two-thirds of survey participants' preference for the word "casual" (64%) over "dignified" (36%). Everyday dishes are casual, convenient and familiar, and that makes them preferable for ordinary use.

Second, we talked with the field groups about Starbucks versus the independent coffee shop, and many participants agreed that, while they might aspire to the ambiance, community and authenticity of the indie coffee house, they usually find themselves at Starbucks. What Starbucks lacks in the intangibles, it makes up for by being convenient and offering a predictable,

Many Millennials aspire to a more traditional church experience, but are more at ease in a modern space.

familiar experience. Millennials might aspire to the rich religious atmosphere and deep-rooted spirituality of Redeemer or St. James, but most would probably find themselves at Buckhead or Willow Creek on any given Sunday.

When we analyzed the results from the word pair section of the survey, we found a couple of interesting countertrends. Several word pairs elicited a reverse preference among one segment—that is, one population segment preferred the opposite word from a majority of Millennials.

▶ 4.2 COUNTERTREND: EXILES' PREFERENCES

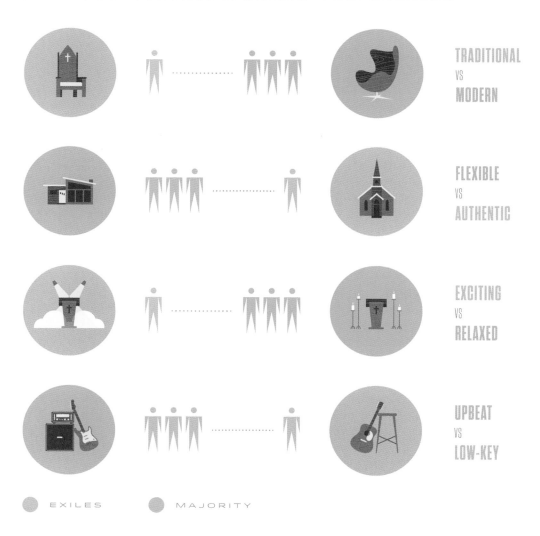

TRADITIONAL
VS
MODERN

FLEXIBLE
VS
AUTHENTIC

EXCITING
VS
RELAXED

UPBEAT
VS
LOW-KEY

EXILES   MAJORITY

• What do you
think are some
ways Millennials'
preferences for
sacred space might
also be applicable to
educational facilities?

• How easily can
Millennials answer
the questions
"Where am I?" and
"What's expected
of me?" from cues
in your learning
environment—and
what effect do you
think more visual
clarity could have on
engagement?

• In addition to
spaces designed for
collaborative and
solitary study, do your
facilities also offer
space for respite and
reflection—and why
do you think (or not
think) this is important
for students?

For example, Exiles—church dropouts who still take their faith seriously but feel caught between church and culture—preferred "traditional" when everyone else preferred "modern," and "authentic" over the majority's preference for "flexible." (See Figure 4.2.) They also preferred "low-key" while a majority in other groups preferred "upbeat." This may reflect their preference for a low-pressure visitor experience.

In another section of the survey, we showed participants images of elements commonly found in North American church buildings, and asked them to choose the one most appealing to them personally. The first series showed four images of different kinds of worship spaces.

Just under half of participants (44%) selected Sanctuary 2 as most appealing with the remaining 56% split almost evenly among the other three images. Those who profess a faith other than Christianity (32%) were more likely than average (20%) to prefer Sanctuary 3; this image is devoid of Christian symbols.

Sanctuary 2 was the "Goldilocks" space for many respondents—not too big, not too small. Just right. It's big enough to retain some anonymity as a visitor—the marginally churched (63%) and those who are not practicing Christians (50%) preferred it more strongly than the average—but small enough to feel part of a community. Parents with children under 18 (50%) also preferred Sanctuary 2 more than average.

This pattern squares with the feedback we got from the field groups: for many, size is a necessary evil rather than a selling point. Participants acknowledged that a successful church would grow and therefore need to increase the size of its services and facilities. But they also expressed a bit of tacit distrust for very large churches. One young man put it starkly: "It seems like a really big business."

The one advantage of a large church is the option to blend in, especially for those who are less than comfortable visiting.

VISUAL CLARITY

"It kinda feels like a bait-and-switch."

This was one of the strongest negative statements we heard from field group participants. It was a comment from an unchurched participant who had toured one of the modern churches. She, along with the rest of her group, was enamored by the creativity of various rooms and common areas, the attention to detail and the quality of the materials. Overall, she said, it was an impressive location.

Later, however, after visiting the downtown cathedral, with its elaborate iconography and traditional layout, she was less impressed with the modern church. She realized how little indication she'd seen that the modern church is

	18%		44%		20%		18%
Male	20%	Male	41%	Male	17%	Male	22%
Female	16%	Female	47%	Female	23%	Female	15%
Married	15%	Married	44%	Married	27%	Married	13%
Unmarried	19%	Unmarried	44%	Unmarried	18%	Unmarried	20%
Single, never married	16%	Single, never married	47%	Single, never married	17%	Single, never married	20%
Children	14%	Children	50%	Children	15%	Children	21%
No children	21%	No children	39%	No children	24%	No children	16%
HS or less	22%	HS or less	39%	HS or less	18%	HS or less	21%
Some college	14%	Some college	49%	Some college	21%	Some college	17%
College Grad	17%	College grad	46%	College grad	22%	College grad	15%
<$40k	20%	<$40k	40%	<$40k	20%	<$40k	20%
$40k - $60k	18%	$40k - $60k	45%	$40k - $60k	20%	$40k - $60k	17%
$60k+	16%	$60k+	47%	$60k+	20%	$60k+	17%
Churched	22%	Churched	39%	Churched	20%	Churched	19%
Marginally churched	15%	Marginally churched	63%	Marginally churched	7%	Marginally churched	16%
Unchurched	17%	Unchurched	42%	Unchurched	23%	Unchurched	19%
Other faith	24%	Other faith	34%	Other faith	32%	Other faith	11%
No faith	20%	No faith	38%	No faith	21%	No faith	20%
White	15%	White	42%	White	22%	White	21%
Black	18%	Black	49%	Black	18%	Black	15%
Hispanic	20%	Hispanic	48%	Hispanic	14%	Hispanic	18%
Nonwhite	21%	Nonwhite	48%	Nonwhite	17%	Nonwhite	15%
Northeast	18%	Northeast	50%	Northeast	14%	Northeast	18%
South	15%	South	39%	South	20%	South	26%
Midwest	17%	Midwest	43%	Midwest	24%	Midwest	16%
West	22%	West	44%	West	19%	West	15%

Barna/CKN. October 2013, N=843 U.S. adults ages 18 to 29 years old. The segmentation percentages above are among Millennials who participated in the study.

a religious institution. The more she thought about it, the more frustrated she became. She felt the cathedral presented itself honestly, while the modern church was trying to pass itself off as something else.

We heard similar perspectives from multiple participants in both cities. Once they viewed the rich religious décor of the cathedrals, they wished there were more of it in the modern facilities.

On the whole, Millennials have a strong preference for unambiguous visual clarity. Practically speaking, field group participants expressed appreciation for clear signage and directions for how and where to find information. More philosophically, Millennials want to be able to answer the questions "Where am I?" and "What's expected of me?" by looking for cues in their surroundings. Cathedrals and traditional churches have such cues in spades, yet modern churches are often designed expressly to be ambiguous.

This is a wise strategy if a church's goal is to reach people for whom "church" is loaded with negative connotations. For example, the seeker-friendly movement set about to attract people who had a negative personal history with traditional churches and wanted something different—so modern churches aimed for different. But this younger generation of seekers doesn't have the same history with traditional churches. Some have grown up with such buildings, but the childhood frame of reference for many others is the modern, un-churchy church facility. Still others have no frame of reference at all. When the field group entered the lobby area of Buckhead Church, a large modern church campus north of downtown Atlanta, one participant asked, "If I came here on Sunday morning, would I have to pay?" That level of unfamiliarity with churches is not rare among Millennials.

They want a church to be open and honest about what it is and about what it is trying to accomplish. Most expect a Christian church to look . . . like a Christian church. When it doesn't, some feel off-balance and perplexed.

Wanting clarity in their church experience is most prevalent among Millennials who are peripherally connected to Christianity or with a community of faith. When we asked survey participants, "How important is it to you that a church building looks like a church?" answers fell somewhat evenly across the spectrum from "very" to "not at all." Six in 10 young adults fell somewhere in the middle, and the overall trend was toward less importance. Skewing higher, however, were the six in 10 notional Christians (59%)—that is, those who self-identify as Christian but are not born again—who said it is somewhat or very important to them that a church looks like a church. This is 12 percentage points higher than the average (47%). A similar proportion of the marginally churched (58%) reported it is somewhat or very important. (Those who are marginally churched have attended a service, other than a funeral or wedding, within the past six months but not within the past month.)

Millennials want a church to be open and honest about what it is and about what it is trying to accomplish.

HOW IMPORTANT IS IT TO YOU THAT A CHURCH BUILDING LOOK LIKE A CHURCH?

6 IN 10

FALL IN THE MIDDLE—SAYING IT IS ONLY SOMEWHAT OR SOMEWHAT NOT IMPORTANT

CATHOLIC	CHURCHED	NOTIONAL CHRISTIAN	PRACTICING CHRISTIAN	HISPANIC	PROTESTANT
73%	60%	59%	59%	57%	53%

 ALL MILLENNIALS
(% VERY OR SOMEWHAT IMPORTANT)

47%

BLACK	OTHER FAITH	WHITE	UNCHURCHED	EVANGELICAL	NO FAITH
51%	43%	43%	38%	28%	20%

In addition to sacred architecture, religious iconography—crosses, stained glass and altars, for example—also play an important role. They connect people to the traditions and history of Christianity. Congregants are connected to the church through the ages, rather than only being connected to each other in the here and now. (This is the longer view of the "communion of saints" referenced in the Apostles' Creed.) Despite much conventional wisdom, young people often place great value on the old way of doing things: witness the resurgence in cloth diapers, gardening and even knitting! Rather than relegating religious symbols to the storage closet, modern churches might rather find innovative ways to incorporate them into their décor.

The second series of images in the survey showed four different altar areas with varying levels of ornamentation and iconography.

▶ Q&A WITH KEVIN MILLER

Kevin Miller is Associate Rector of Church of the Resurrection in Wheaton, Illinois (www. churchrez.org). He is a featured preacher on PreachingToday.com and a contributor to LeadershipJournal.net.

What are three to five tips or best practices you could offer to churches who are considering a refresh on their spaces?

• Put Millennials on the fundraising team.
• Put Millennials on the design team.
• Visit community restaurants and stores frequented by Millennials.
• Think "organic" in materials and color palette.
• Add tons of space for strollers and for toddler play.

How can churches meet this draw among Millennials toward traditional spaces with their equal desire for comfort?

The winning combination is "cathedral" for your worship space and "coffee shop" for your gathering space. But it's important that your worship theology and practice is right for a cathedral-like space. Does it draw on traditional sources? Does it incorporate any music written before this century?

Male	22%	Male	30%	Male	38%	Male	10%
Female	16%	Female	36%	Female	36%	Female	12%
Married	30%	Married	32%	Married	26%	Married	11%
Unmarried	16%	Unmarried	33%	Unmarried	40%	Unmarried	10%
Single, never married	16%	Single, never married	32%	Single, never married	42%	Single, never married	10%
Children	18%	Children	34%	Children	36%	Children	12%
No children	20%	No children	32%	No children	38%	No children	10%
HS or less	21%	HS or less	30%	HS or less	37%	HS or less	11%
Some college	19%	Some college	36%	Some college	35%	Some college	10%
College Grad	15%	College grad	33%	College grad	40%	College grad	12%
<$40k	17%	<$40k	31%	<$40k	41%	<$40k	11%
$40k - $60k	25%	$40k - $60k	36%	$40k - $60k	27%	$40k - $60k	12%
$60k+	19%	$60k+	33%	$60k+	38%	$60k+	11%
Churched	17%	Churched	37%	Churched	34%	Churched	13%
Marginally churched	18%	Marginally churched	32%	Marginally churched	41%	Marginally churched	8%
Unchurched	21%	Unchurched	31%	Unchurched	38%	Unchurched	11%
Other faith	51%	Other faith	25%	Other faith	22%	Other faith	2%
No faith	29%	No faith	23%	No faith	40%	No faith	8%
White	21%	White	38%	White	34%	White	7%
Black	12%	Black	43%	Black	25%	Black	21%
Hispanic	19%	Hispanic	14%	Hispanic	54%	Hispanic	14%
Nonwhite	16%	Nonwhite	26%	Nonwhite	40%	Nonwhite	17%
Northeast	18%	Northeast	29%	Northeast	34%	Northeast	19%
South	20%	South	29%	South	46%	South	6%
Midwest	19%	Midwest	40%	Midwest	30%	Midwest	11%
West	20%	West	29%	West	42%	West	9%

Barna/CKN, October 2013, N=843 U.S. adults ages 18 to 29 years old. The segmentation percentages above are among Millennials who participated in the study.

Altars 2 (33%) and 3 (37%) were the overall favorites. Both are unambiguously Christian and are more traditional in appearance than 4. Analysis of faith and demographic segments reveals a few interesting trends. Nearly half of non-mainline Protestants (48%) preferred Altar 2, with an even stronger preference among evangelicals (55%). By contrast, Catholics (63%) and notional Christians (48%) were more likely than average to prefer Altar 3. About half of those professing a faith other than Christianity (51%) found Altar 1 most appealing—it lacks overt Christian iconography—and three in 10 of those with no faith (29%) also chose Altar 1. Both these proportions were much higher than the average (19%).

Looking at ethnic, age and other demographics, we find that Hispanic

▶ Q&A WITH DEREK DEGROOT

Derek DeGroot, AIA, is an architect for Aspen Group, a design-build firm in the Midwest that works exclusively with churches. He is passionate about creating physical spaces that connect people, and he speaks and writes regularly on this topic. You can find some of his work at AspenGroup. com.

Why do you think it's important for churches to consider their space and architecture? How do these elements impact worship and community?

As the missional renaissance kicked up dirt over the last decade, a school of thought formed around the idea that spaces aren't important. Instead, minimalists contended we should maximize resources into our missions and ministry, saving whatever we could in facility costs. Recently, however, more churches are realizing that the best approach is a balance of stewardship and space that enhances ministry.

A building can help connect people who have never met. A building can impact our emotional experience. It can propel us to action or give us much-needed rest. A building is like fertilizer: Ministry can flourish in a building that enhances it. Churches that consider their spaces important are able to use them to improve ministry, connect people and enhance the worship experience. In

a world that's increasingly modular, our buildings and spaces offer an incredible, physical opportunity to show people what our vision is.

Why do you think many Millennials gravitate toward more traditional worship spaces?

The cathedral is powerfully symbolic, connecting our world to the one above. But it's also a common symbol of church in the secular world, frequently featured on TV shows, movies and in literature. Perhaps this standard Hollywood depiction makes the traditional church a standout symbol of Christianity, where the modern day church works so hard to blend into its culture. With this in mind, it's easy to say we need more cathedrals because so many unchurched people are fond of them, but that's not practical given modern church programming and budgets. Instead, churches can focus on designing for clarity. Good design can make it crystal clear who they are, what they believe and what they are there to do.

participants strongly preferred Altar 3 (54%), while twice as many blacks (21%) as the national average (11%) found Altar 4 appealing. There seem to be significant regional differences, as well: Midwesterners were more likely to prefer Altar 2 (40%) and Southerners more likely to choose 3 (46%). Married people (30%) and adults ages 25 to 29 (25%) were more likely than average to find Altar 1 appealing.

These patterns illustrate most Millennials' overall preference for a straightforward, overtly Christian style of imagery—as long as it doesn't look too institutional or corporate. Not only do such settings physically direct one's attention to the divine, they also provide the rich context of church history as a backdrop for worship.

Religious iconography connects people to the traditions and history of Christianity.

What do you see as the biggest barrier or problem for churches when it comes to their space?
Budgets are and may always be the biggest hurdle to overcome in creating great space. Most churches are pressed for funds, and their limited dollars are given in great faith by many generous people.

So how do you create great spaces on a shoestring budget? First, concentrate on one or two areas and make them special. Instead of spreading funds equally throughout the facility, make your spaces utilitarian in general but go the extra mile in a few areas. Keep your structures simple, and instead invest more of your building budget on finishes, furniture and technology that display great thought and care. Limit expensive materials to a few choice facades or a special landscape feature. Better yet, there are thousands of buildings begging to be reused and repurposed. Creative designers can do unthinkable transformations of car dealerships, retail spaces or warehouses that dot our landscape. Instead of spending dollars on site work, parking and structures, spend your money on outfitting these existing spaces in new ways. Oftentimes you'll get twice the value at half the cost! Talk about good stewardship.

"I could come here during lunch to pray."

The statement was a surprise. First, the young woman did not even attend a church, and was not someone we would expect to undertake an impromptu prayer session during the middle of her workday.

Second, she said it in a tiny traditional chapel just a few feet from a busy downtown Chicago street. Opaque windows, hard wooden benches, burning candles and a low-vaulted ceiling completed the grotto's décor. It was hardly the place we might expect an unchurched 24-year-old woman to feel at peace.

What did this little chapel, with its overtly religious décor, hard floors and harder seats provide that the luxurious modern facility in the suburbs did not?

As we discussed above, many of our churches today are not defined by form but by function—by the activities that go on inside. And while that's not altogether a bad thing, some Millennials feel something has been lost along the way.

Our churches are places of action, not places of rest; spaces to do rather than spaces to be. The activities, of course, are designed to connect people with God and each other—and some Millennials hope for that, too—but many just want an opportunity to explore spiritual life on their own terms, free to decide for themselves when to stay on the edges of a church experience and when to fully enter in.

When we walked into the cathedrals, participants sat down. Churched or unchurched, Christian or non-, they intuitively understood they were in a place where it was fine to sit . . . and do nothing. Is it a wonder we see an uptick in Millennials seeking out liturgical forms of worship? Or that Millennials who know about Lent are more likely than their parents to practice it? (And often what they give up is technology—to find that slower pace, if only for a few weeks.)

The desire for space to reflect came up again and again among participants, and many connected their desire for peace directly to their expectations or hopes for church. Our culture is highly fragmented and frenetic, and there are few places to take a breather and gain much-needed perspective. When half of Millennials check their phone first thing in the morning and last thing at night; when many become physically anxious if they don't have their phone on them at any given time; when #FOMO is both a cry for help and a badge of honor; when young moms scour Pinterest for fun ideas and end up feeling inadequate because their kid's lunch doesn't feature homegrown cabbage wraps shaped like algebraic equations (so little Johnny can develop math skills and go to Harvard Business School and take his company public) . . . it's no wonder our churches offer what people think they want: more to do, more to see.

Yet that's exactly the opposite of what many young adults crave when it comes to sacred space.

Your church. Is it a place of energy and activity?

> Many Millennials connect their desire for peace directly to their expectations or hopes for church.

What are three to five tips or best practices you could offer to churches who are considering a refresh on their spaces?

• Add video projection and upgrade the AVL to enhance the teaching and worship experience
• Create large lobbies and expand narrow halls
• Convert church parlors, fellowship halls and gymnasiums into relationally inviting rooms that foster community, like Wi-Fi cafes, conversation pits and conference rooms
• Transform children's spaces into cutting-edge environments that are open, colorful and secure

What shifts have you seen in your field over the last few decades? Is there something churches can and should learn from those shifts?

• The technological revolution has extended church impact beyond the walls of a building and its geographic location
• The multisite revolution liberated churches from unsustainable mega-campuses
• The economic recession liberated churches from expensive building campaigns
• The decline in church attendance is forcing churches to build community-centric, multi-purpose and environmentally friendly facilities
• The church planting resurgence is retrofitting existing commercial facilities and building smaller church facilities with multiple venues.
• The church merger trend is redeeming and recycling existing church buildings for renewed use

What do you see as the biggest barrier or problem for churches when it comes to their space and/ or architecture? What are some ways to overcome this hurdle?

The historic value of church attendance that once permeated American culture is receding. There has been a major cultural shift away from church attendance and the value of church buildings. Church buildings that were once seen as an asset to a local community are increasingly being viewed more as a liability. In the eyes of non-churchgoers, church buildings take money off the tax rolls, cause traffic problems and create noise issues. As a result there is an increasing community resistance to churches buying land and building facilities, especially large facilities. To win the hearts of the secular community, church buildings will have to be multi-purpose facilities that not only serve the church family but also the broader local community. New church buildings going up today need to be smaller, multipurpose, multi-venue, community-centric and environmentally friendly "green" buildings. And though church facilities will tend to be more utilitarian than the cathedrals of the past, they also must be aesthetically inviting.

Jim Tomberlin is founder and senior strategist of MultiSite Solutions, a company dedicated to assisting churches in extending their impact through multiple locations. He is the "MultiSite Guy," the nationally recognized expert on multisite church, and the "Merger Guru," with nearly a third of his consulting involving church mergers. He is the author of 125 Tips for MultiSite Churches, Better Together: Making Church Mergers Work *and* Church Locality: New Rules for Church Buildings in a Multisite, Church Planting and Giga-Church World.

• How much
attention do you pay
to the facilities where
Millennial workers
contribute to your
organization—and
how might their
preferences for sacred
space beneficially
inform your work-
space ethos?

• What does the
design and décor of
your workspace say
about the culture of
your organization—
and is it in line with
the culture you are
trying to create?

• What are some
ways you can bring
the outdoors into your
workspace?

Do you offer all sorts of choices for those who want a vibrant faith experience? That's all well and good. But when do people stop their labors—even their spiritual labors? Where do they go to experience Jesus's invitation, "Come unto me, all ye who are weary and heavy laden, and I will give you rest"?

NATURE

Our field participants couldn't get enough of nature. At each location, the groups as a whole gravitated toward windows and other areas with plenty of natural light. They expressed appreciation for pleasant landscaping, not just as decorative but also functional, setting the stage for community and communion. As we've described, St. James Cathedral boasts a tiny courtyard, lush with plants and a small labyrinth, just steps from a bustling downtown street. Chicago participants were delighted by the peaceful nature oasis; several—like the unchurched young woman mentioned earlier—said that if they worked or lived nearby, they would enjoy visiting on a regular basis to pray, meditate or spend a few moments in quiet reflection.

While nothing tops the real thing, even fake nature was enjoyed by our focus-groups-on-wheels. The children's area at Buckhead Church features a variety of oversized plastic plants and insects on walls and ceilings, and these fun, natural touches were well-reviewed by the group. Likewise, at Willow Creek, a large, decorative "chandelier" made of wooden leaves hanging in a breezeway garnered favorable comments.

Our findings reveal two core questions churches should ask about their facilities. First, how do we bring the outside in? It might be as simple as a large window over a well-landscaped vista or as elaborate as a walled-in courtyard with a water sculpture and mediation benches. Maybe a stone accent wall instead of wallpaper, or bamboo flooring instead of carpet. How can the inside of our church reflect the shapes, textures and colors of its natural surroundings?

Second, how do we bring the inside out? Field participants showed a strong, consistent preference for personal reflection and prayer in an outdoor setting. Some indicated they would rather meet friends outside, as well. Many churches think of their facility as everything inside the walls, but it is worth considering how we might make better use of our external spaces. Instead of using landscaping simply as a frame for the building, could we use it as a legitimate ministry space—a sacred place in its own right?

The third series of images in our national survey showed four images of nature brought into the church space. Most respondents preferred images with greater realism and more immersion into the outdoors.

	9%		15%		15%		62%
Male	8%	Male	14%	Male	18%	Male	60%
Female	10%	Female	15%	Female	11%	Female	64%
Married	7%	Married	13%	Married	16%	Married	64%
Unmarried	10%	Unmarried	15%	Unmarried	14%	Unmarried	61%
Single, never married	9%	Single, never married	15%	Single, never married	14%	Single, never married	61%
Children	11%	Children	15%	Children	15%	Children	58%
No children	7%	No children	14%	No children	14%	No children	65%
HS or less	10%	HS or less	11%	HS or less	20%	HS or less	59%
Some college	10%	Some college	15%	Some college	11%	Some college	64%
College Grad	6%	College grad	21%	College grad	9%	College grad	64%
<$40k	9%	<$40k	11%	<$40k	15%	<$40k	65%
$40k - $60k	9%	$40k - $60k	14%	$40k - $60k	18%	$40k - $60k	60%
$60k+	9%	$60k+	18%	$60k+	13%	$60k+	60%
Churched	14%	Churched	6%	Churched	21%	Churched	59%
Marginally churched	5%	Marginally churched	25%	Marginally churched	20%	Marginally churched	51%
Unchurched	8%	Unchurched	17%	Unchurched	9%	Unchurched	67%
Other faith	9%	Other faith	14%	Other faith	33%	Other faith	44%
No faith	4%	No faith	22%	No faith	5%	No faith	69%
White	8%	White	14%	White	11%	White	67%
Black	9%	Black	9%	Black	30%	Black	52%
Hispanic	11%	Hispanic	17%	Hispanic	19%	Hispanic	53%
Nonwhite	10%	Nonwhite	14%	Nonwhite	20%	Nonwhite	56%
Northeast	5%	Northeast	15%	Northeast	18%	Northeast	61%
South	7%	South	14%	South	10%	South	69%
Midwest	15%	Midwest	12%	Midwest	12%	Midwest	62%
West	6%	West	19%	West	19%	West	57%

Barna/CKN, October 2013, N=843 U.S. adults ages 18 to 29 years old. The segmentation percentages above are among Millennials who participated in the study.

Nature 4, the garden path, was the favorite by far, with 62% choosing it as most appealing; a majority in nearly every population segment preferred it. Catholics (74%), those with no faith (69%), notional Christians (69%) and the unchurched (67%) were even more likely than average to choose 4. While just 9% of all adults chose Nature 1—the more child-oriented paper cutout of a tree—one-quarter of evangelicals (24%) and about one in six born-again Christians (17%) found it most appealing.

Millennials' enthusiasm for the outdoors was also obvious in the majority preference for nature scenes in the image series we explored in chapter 1, "Culture." Nearly two-thirds (64%) chose the tree-shaded bench as illustrative of the statement "feels like home," and more than half (52%) preferred the window-facing desk as the best illustration of "a place I would like to work." (See chapter 1 for these images and more thorough analysis.)

The final series of pictures showed four different images of church windows. We were particularly interested in this topic because we had identified two contradictory findings from our field groups: they loved big, open windows (nature), but they also loved stained glass (visual clarity). What would happen when we pitted the two against each other?

Windows 1 and 4 tied as most appealing, with both garnering 35% of participants' votes. This is a drastic split; 1 is the most modern, least "churchy" of the images, while 4 is the most ornate and traditional. These survey results are consistent with our field group findings: Millennials like both! So why not embrace both types of windows? We saw a space with both in Church of the Redeemer in downtown Atlanta. It has a small prayer chapel with an ornate stained glass image of Jesus at the front, flanked by two large, open windows. The overall effect is very pleasant, and was noticed with appreciation by our field participants.

Middle-class young adults were more likely (45%) than average to prefer Window 1, as were Midwesterners (41%). This was also the case, by a wide margin, with those adhering to non-Christian faiths (61%). On the other side, Catholics (55%), residents of the West (44%) and Hispanics (44%) were all more likely than average to find Window 4 most appealing. (There is likely significant crossover among these three segments.)

Male	34%	Male	9%	Male	21%	Male	36%
Female	36%	Female	9%	Female	22%	Female	34%
Married	47%	Married	8%	Married	18%	Married	27%
Unmarried	32%	Unmarried	9%	Unmarried	23%	Unmarried	37%
Single, never married	28%	Single, never married	8%	Single, never married	25%	Single, never married	38%
Children	37%	Children	7%	Children	22%	Children	34%
No children	33%	No children	11%	No children	21%	No children	36%
HS or less	36%	HS or less	6%	HS or less	22%	HS or less	37%
Some college	36%	Some college	10%	Some college	21%	Some college	34%
College Grad	31%	College grad	12%	College grad	23%	College grad	34%
<$40k	36%	<$40k	7%	<$40k	21%	<$40k	36%
$40k - $60k	45%	$40k - $60k	6%	$40k - $60k	17%	$40k - $60k	32%
$60k+	30%	$60k+	11%	$60k+	24%	$60k+	35%
Churched	40%	Churched	6%	Churched	23%	Churched	32%
Marginally churched	31%	Marginally churched	4%	Marginally churched	28%	Marginally churched	37%
Unchurched	33%	Unchurched	11%	Unchurched	21%	Unchurched	35%
Other faith	61%	Other faith	6%	Other faith	12%	Other faith	21%
No faith	38%	No faith	9%	No faith	13%	No faith	39%
White	36%	White	11%	White	20%	White	32%
Black	41%	Black	2%	Black	27%	Black	29%
Hispanic	29%	Hispanic	4%	Hispanic	22%	Hispanic	44%
Nonwhite	34%	Nonwhite	5%	Nonwhite	24%	Nonwhite	38%
Northeast	30%	Northeast	10%	Northeast	22%	Northeast	21%
South	29%	South	13%	South	21%	South	23%
Midwest	41%	Midwest	9%	Midwest	25%	Midwest	25%
West	35%	West	3%	West	18%	West	44%

Barna/CKN, October 2013. N=843 U.S. adults ages 18 to 29 years old. The segmentation percentages above are among Millennials who participated in the study.

Again and again, we have circled back to five reasons Millennials stay connected to a faith community: cultural discernment, mentoring, vocational discipleship and life-shaping relationships with God and other people. Rarely do these happen by accident, at least not for long. Faith-centered organizations must make deliberate choices about their structures—their culture, ministry, leadership and buildings—to facilitate these essentials.

The satirical "news" website *The Onion* published a story a few years ago under the headline, "Area Teen Accidentally Enters Teen Center." It reads:

> In a moment of confusion, area teenager Eric Dooley briefly walked into a local teen outreach center Tuesday, a place that neither he nor any of his teenaged friends would ever knowingly enter. "Oh, geez. I'm sorry," the 15-year-old said as he quickly assessed the four battered foosball tables, outdated PlayStation console, overly friendly counselor, and garish orange and purple paint scheme—all intended to appeal to him— before exiting the facility in less than six seconds.[1]

All too often our churches make the same mistakes as that fictional youth center. We try so hard to make our spaces "edgy" and "real" that they become caricatures and clichés. They end up repelling the very people we are trying to engage.

It's tempting to oversimplify the relationship between Millennials and sacred space. For instance, it might be easy to believe such a place needs to look ultra modern or chic to appeal to teens and young adults. But the truth, like so much about this generation, is more complicated—refreshingly so. Most Millennials don't look for a church facility that caters to the whims of pop culture. They want a community that calls them to deeper meaning.

Does that sound like your community of faith? If you're in the business of following Jesus, of course it does! So let your facilities reflect your church's calling to connect with God and each other.

There are myriad ways to design sacred and communal spaces that call people of all ages to deeper relationships with God, self and others. No two churches will (or should) incorporate them all in the same way. There is no cookie-cutter, mass-production solution for welcoming Millennials to your space, but there are questions your community can keep in mind as you build to include the whole church body:

- How do our facilities present visual cues? Can people easily answer the questions "Where am I?" and "What's expected of me?"

- How do our facilities offer respite from the outside world? Can people find a place of peace that is accessible and comfortable?

Let your facilities reflect your church's calling to connect with God and each other.

- How do our facilities connect to Christian history and traditions? What symbols or design elements evoke a sense of the sacred and tell the story of God's actions in the world?

- How do our facilities integrate elements of nature? How can we bring the outside in and take the inside out?

Designing or redesigning our structures in such a way that Millennials are welcomed into our community is not a matter of trendiness or of keeping up with cultural fads. (In fact, many of the choices we make with younger people in mind may require us to swim against the wider cultural stream.) Rather, putting the needs of the next generation ahead of our own preferences is an act of service.

After he had washed his disciples' feet, Jesus asked them, "Do you understand what I was doing? You call me 'Teacher' and 'Lord,' and you are right, because that's what I am. And since I, your Lord and Teacher, have washed your feet, you ought to wash each other's feet. I have given you an example to follow. Do as I have done to you. . . . Now that you know these things, God will bless you for doing them" (John 13:12-15,17, NLT).

Cultural discernment, intergenerational friendships, reverse mentoring, vocational discipleship, and an experience of and connection with Jesus are five reasons Millennials go to and stay in church. How well do your facilities, inside and out, allow you to facilitate these important outcomes?

NOTE:

[1] "Area Teen Accidently Enters Teen Center," *The Onion*, January 7, 2009. http://www.theonion.com/articles/area-teen-accidentally-enters-teen-center,6515/ (accessed May 2014).

Sara Joy Proppe works in real estate development in Minneapolis, where she oversees a variety of mixed-use and historic rehab projects. With degrees in English Literature and Urban Planning, she spends much of her time mulling over and exploring how city design shapes the stories lived in the spaces and places we inhabit. In particular, she is passionate about educating churches on what it means to steward the built environment for the common good, and how Christian leaders can engage in city planning and development. Sara Joy shares her work by writing on such topics and speaking to congregations in the Twin Cities.

Why do you think it's important for churches to consider their space and architecture? How do these elements impact worship and community?

God created us as physical beings who occupy real space and time and are deeply affected by our environment. Not only that, the Genesis mandate to fill the earth gives us the honor of being co-creators with God in our story. Part of redeeming the human story requires stewarding our physical setting for the common good, and the built environment (including church buildings!) is a fundamental component. In the book of Jeremiah, God tells the Israelites in exile to build houses and plant gardens even in the midst of not being truly "at home." Likewise, we are called to put down roots in a particular place and physically invest in a community. To answer this call in our modern context, I believe a church needs to consider its space and architecture, particularly with regard to how they interact with the geographic context and community around them. The physical design of their building, by either exuding a fortress mentality or an invitation to participation and wonder, influences the type of interaction a church has with the surrounding community. For example, a church property can be designed for people or for cars—consider the sea of parking lots that surround most modern church buildings. Instead, churches could situate their building frontage close to sidewalks and streets with clearly accessible pedestrian paths to the front door. This allows people more interaction with the building and clear visibility of where to enter, and integrates the church building into the larger community.

Historically, churches were situated in the center of town, and their ornate architecture signified a transcendent or "otherness" function. While a church building was not a place of everydayness, its physical embeddedness within the larger built environment made it a visible and integrated part of the community. Modern churches that choose to build on large lots at the edge of town are demonstrably isolating themselves from the community and are often less accessible to community members because of the distance they have to travel. This type of "commuter" church building does not invite its members to invest in one geographic place together (ideally around the church building). Consistent communal interaction among attendees throughout the week is weakened. I believe these realities hinder a church community from putting down roots in a particular place, and work against our call to steward the built environment for the common good.

Why do you think many Millennials gravitate toward more traditional worship spaces? How can churches respond to this even as they try to offer comfortable spaces, which Millennials also appreciate?

The built environment orients us in a particular place. This is why Millenials gravitate toward more traditional worship spaces. They are hungry for rootedness and community. Having grown up in an era of ubiquitous McDonalds, Wal-Marts and housing tracts, placelessness dominates much of their human experience. Modern development patterns, driven by chain stores and highway systems, have made one place indistinguishable from another. In contrast, places imbued with particularity root us in memory, connecting us to the places we inhabit and to one another. Corporate memory is fundamental to community formation. In traditional worship spaces, Millenials are connected to the shared story with generations who have gone before them. As beings created for community, we thrive most when we are rooted together in a larger narrative. Despite all the virtual connections Millienials have through social media, I believe they are eager for tangible, physical community. A traditional church building that echoes a history of community resonates with that desire.

The Barna study reveals the contradiction many Millenials feel: a desire for comfortable anonymity yet an affinity for traditional communal religious spaces. The common approach of many modern churches is to err on the side of comfort and anonymity, stripping away religious elements and designing spaces for activities—but we should not throw the baby out with the bathwater. The Barna study notes, "Millenials want to be able to answer the question 'Where am I?'" Answering that question requires being oriented by and rooted in a communal history. Our church buildings should reflect that history in creative ways.

INTERVIEW WITH
ED BAHLER, CKN

What needs did you see among churches and church leaders that inspired you to start the Cornerstone Knowledge Network? What's the mission?
The Cornerstone Knowledge Network (CKN) was founded by Aspen Group and Cogun, two church design and construction firms that build churches in competing markets and yet share a heart for ministry. Both Aspen and Cogun believe that we can do more for the church by learning and sharing knowledge, rather than hiding and hoarding information for our individual business gain.

Our shared vision—to create meaningful knowledge to help the church—gave birth to CKN, a mutually created initiative that has led to a variety of research and learning events since 2004. The research we do through CKN provides insight into how facility design, as well as culture, leadership and ministry, affect and shape the church.

Why do this kind of research?
We partnered with Barna Group on the "Making Space for Millennials" research project for several reasons. First, Barna is one of the leading experts on Millennials. We wanted to partner with an organization that was deeply immersed in understanding the cultural trends that set this generation apart from its forebears and how the unique attributes of today's young adults are affecting the church.

Second, we know that church leaders are struggling with how to recapture the hearts, minds and souls of Millennials. As David Kinnaman's extensive research and writing on Millennials shows, churches have largely lost this generation of young adults, and the fallout of this mass exodus will have far-reaching, long-term consequences if churches don't wake up and pay attention to what's happening in the culture.

Third, at CKN we invest in research to discover what factors, such as facilities or ministry design, impact a church's success. So for instance, because Millennials are a large, influential demographic, we wanted to learn what factors in churches help young people connect with God and which ones push them further away. Not only did we come away with a deeper understanding of the cultural trends related to Millennials, but we also have a better handle on the ministry challenges young adults pose for churches, as well as the leadership traits that are required to shepherd this generation.

Additionally, all of this data and discovery is especially relevant on a practical level for our architects and designers. As we guide and assist churches to create ministry space that will have a meaningful spiritual impact, we can draw from the research's findings to help shape churches' decisions on what types of facilities to build.

It's the alignment of these four factors—culture, leadership, ministry, and facilities—that helps position a church for radical ministry impact. This is the driving force behind why we invest in research. It's not about having the right answers—it's about making sure we're having the right conversations with churches before they build.

As we walk with a church and discover its unique heartbeat for God's people—its core values and DNA—we can use research like "Making Space for Millennials" to help ensure that churches build the right ministry space for lasting impact.

What are the main findings from the study that are changing how you approach your mission?
The "Making Space for Millennials" study helped deepen our understanding on at least four key points: visual clarity, respite, nature and modularity. As the chapters in this monograph reveal, there is much we can learn about young adults and their desire to connect with God and others in meaningful ways.

Beyond giving us clues about how to attract and retain more Millennials in the church, this research fans the flames of our passion to inspire and equip churches to, in turn, inspire and equip the next generation to lead the church in ways we—and they—can't even imagine today. In order to do this, we need to first help Millennials find their way back to God, and second, make room for them once they return.

We're privileged to join you on the journey of discovering how to better reach God's people.

Ed Bahler, CEO of Aspen Group
On behalf of the Cornerstone Knowledge Network

	Total	Gender		Age	
Table 1 | Visual Poll Part 1 Which picture best illustrates the statement ... ?		Male	Female	< 25	25 - 29
Feels like home					
Beach	16%	16%	16%	17%	15%
City	12	13	11	12	12
Fall	64	62	66	64	64
Road trip	8	9	7	7	8
A place I would like to work					
Traditional office	22	22	21	22	21
Cozy office	8	5	10	9	6
Home office	52	52	52	50	54
Open space office	19	21	17	20	18
Feels like present-day Christianity					
Worshipping hands	23	25	21	27	17
Finger pointing	37	35	38	35	40
Helping homeless	24	24	24	24	24
Picketer	16	16	16	14	19
Feels like my family					
Friends at cafe	25	28	23	31	17
Friends at party	22	23	21	23	20
Holding hands	42	37	47	36	51
Online connection	11	13	10	10	13
What church should be in the world					
Bible study	48	48	48	49	45
Gym	7	10	4	7	7
Hospital	12	12	13	14	10
Watering can	33	30	36	29	38

	Ethnicity				Faith Practice				Faith Tribe				Churched Status		
	White	Black	Hispanic	All non-white	Practicing Christian	Non-practicing Christian	Other faith	No faith	Prodigals	Nomads	Exiles	Faithfuls	Churched	Marginally	Unchurched
	17%	10%	20%	16%	20%	12%	28%	12%	19%	17%	15%	18%	18%	5%	16%
	8	20	17	18	8	9	17	20	21	9	3	14	8	7	15
	69	67	52	58	67	71	47	58	55	67	75	61	68	80	61
	7	3	11	9	6	8	9	10	5	6	7	8	7	8	8
	20	30	19	24	20	25	24	17	22	28	24	13	20	17	24
	7	10	8	8	7	8	9	8	13	5	5	10	6	6	9
	56	35	51	47	57	49	47	54	50	50	58	54	57	52	48
	17	25	22	22	17	19	20	22	16	17	13	23	14	25	19
	21	33	22	25	37	19	19	21	17	17	39	27	30	27	18
	36	42	39	39	22	42	40	41	37	45	27	26	28	42	41
	26	16	23	22	34	29	13	10	11	25	28	39	35	22	19
	18	10	16	14	7	11	28	29	35	13	6	8	8	9	22
	30	19	15	19	23	24	26	33	27	26	20	30	23	33	25
	20	23	25	24	19	23	18	19	20	27	21	16	20	14	22
	41	40	50	45	46	45	47	33	40	40	44	45	47	43	41
	10	19	10	12	13	9	8	15	13	8	14	9	11	10	12
	42	64	55	57	60	53	32	29	28	58	63	54	58	46	42
	7	3	10	8	3	8	9	6	10	8	1	8	5	3	9
	17	6	5	5	12	11	9	17	16	11	13	11	12	25	10
	35	27	30	31	25	27	50	48	46	24	23	27	26	26	39

	Total	Gender		Age	
Table 2 | Descriptions of the Church Thinking about the state of present-day Christianity in America, how much do you think that the following statements describe the Christian community?		Male	Female	< 25	25 - 29
The people at church are hypocritical					
A lot	26%	25%	26%	19%	34%
Somewhat	40	37	44	42	38
Not too much	21	26	17	25	16
Not at all	13	13	13	13	12
The people at church are tolerant of those with different beliefs					
A lot	11	13	8	11	11
Somewhat	35	34	36	36	33
Not too much	33	32	33	35	29
Not at all	22	20	23	18	27
The church is relevant for my life					
A lot	25	27	24	28	23
Somewhat	29	27	31	28	31
Not too much	19	18	19	20	17
Not at all	27	28	26	25	29
I feel like I can "be myself" at church					
A lot	20	22	19	20	20
Somewhat	29	28	29	29	28
Not too much	24	22	27	25	23
Not at all	27	28	25	26	28
The church is overprotective of teenagers					
A lot	10	12	9	8	13
Somewhat	27	25	29	26	29
Not too much	43	41	45	45	40
Not at all	20	23	17	21	19

	Ethnicity				Faith Practice				Faith Tribe				Churched Status		
	White	Black	Hispanic	All non-white	Practicing Christian	Non-practicing Christian	Other faith	No faith	Prodigals	Nomads	Exiles	Faithfuls	Churched	Marginally	Unchurched
	25%	19%	30%	26%	13%	18%	40%	52%	57%	23%	17%	7%	11%	26%	34%
	43	43	31	37	35	48	36	34	30	50	36	37	41	39	41
	22	26	17	21	30	24	11	10	8	18	29	36	30	28	15
	11	11	22	17	22	11	13	5	5	9	18	20	18	7	10
	7	17	18	15	27	7	11	1	5	6	23	23	24	4	5
	39	30	28	30	43	41	39	13	15	36	47	43	46	48	27
	35	27	31	30	23	35	21	44	31	43	22	23	23	29	38
	19	26	23	25	6	18	30	41	49	15	8	11	7	18	30
	23	38	29	28	76	15	20	1	5	13	71	46	61	17	9
	25	32	41	35	20	47	19	3	8	44	23	46	31	47	24
	23	14	10	13	4	27	16	18	19	32	6	6	8	32	22
	29	17	20	23	1	11	46	79	68	11	*	2	1	4	45
	17	28	27	25	45	16	19	2	6	13	41	35	42	16	10
	30	20	27	26	38	36	19	10	11	35	35	45	39	31	23
	25	27	25	24	11	35	25	18	22	37	20	14	14	46	26
	28	25	20	25	6	13	38	70	60	15	4	6	6	7	41
	9	12	14	12	7	5	15	21	28	5	13	1	5	6	14
	25	22	35	31	29	26	34	24	27	29	26	34	30	32	24
	47	45	32	39	32	54	37	38	28	54	31	41	38	49	45
	20	21	19	19	32	15	15	18	16	12	30	24	27	13	16

	Total	Gender		Age	
Table 2 | Cont'd		Male	Female	< 25	25 - 29
The faith and teachings I encounter at church seem rather shallow					
A lot	12%	13%	12%	11%	14%
Somewhat	26	26	26	23	30
Not too much	30	29	31	33	26
Not at all	32	33	31	33	30
The church seems to reject much of what science tells us about the world					
A lot	25	26	25	22	31
Somewhat	38	37	40	38	38
Not too much	22	19	25	25	18
Not at all	14	19	10	16	13
The church seems too much like an exclusive club					
A lot	14	16	11	11	17
Somewhat	30	25	34	31	28
Not too much	29	28	30	31	26
Not at all	28	30	25	27	29
The church is not a safe place to express doubts					
A lot	16	16	17	16	17
Somewhat	29	27	31	29	30
Not too much	28	29	27	26	30
Not at all	27	28	25	29	23
The church is a place to find answers to live a meaningful life					
A lot	30	29	32	32	28
Somewhat	35	36	35	35	36
Not too much	18	18	19	20	16
Not at all	16	17	15	13	20

	Ethnicity				Faith Practice				Faith Tribe				Churched Status		
	White	Black	Hispanic	All non-white	Practicing Christian	Non-practicing Christian	Other faith	No faith	Prodigals	Nomads	Exiles	Faithfuls	Churched	Marginally	Unchurched
	12%	5%	13%	12%	4%	5%	31%	29%	42%	6%	2%	5%	7%	2%	18%
	27	15	27	24	17	24	24	41	38	29	16	21	18	24	31
	31	45	23	30	25	42	18	18	13	38	31	32	27	52	29
	30	35	38	34	54	29	26	13	7	27	51	41	49	22	23
	25	25	24	26	14	17	37	49	52	20	16	15	15	19	34
	35	40	44	42	29	44	40	37	35	52	31	29	32	45	40
	24	21	19	20	26	29	12	8	7	23	23	30	28	29	17
	16	14	12	12	31	10	11	6	6	4	30	25	26	7	9
	10	13	21	18	11	9	20	25	33	13	12	7	9	9	17
	29	32	21	30	20	31	39	31	30	33	22	17	21	34	33
	32	30	28	25	29	33	16	24	18	32	27	38	32	27	28
	29	25	30	27	40	27	26	20	19	22	39	38	38	30	22
	15	18	17	19	4	11	32	36	42	10	6	10	9	14	22
	29	21	32	29	24	31	31	28	23	36	24	22	24	37	31
	29	36	22	26	28	34	19	17	16	32	28	33	31	34	25
	27	26	29	26	45	24	18	19	19	22	42	35	37	16	23
	26	47	40	38	67	28	26	2	4	27	62	48	59	28	16
	39	29	32	31	28	49	23	22	29	46	33	46	33	44	35
	19	17	13	18	4	19	30	28	27	24	5	2	6	24	24
	17	7	16	14	2	5	22	49	41	3	*	4	2	5	25

	Total	Gender		Age		
Table 3 | Ideal Church: Word Preferences Take a look at the following pairs of words. For each pair, select a word that describes your "ideal" church. Even if you don't attend anywhere currently, we still want to know which word appeals to you more for a church.		Male	Female	< 25	25 - 29	
Classic	67%	67%	68%	68%	66%	
Trendy	33	33	32	32	34	
Modern	60	56	64	61	59	
Traditional	40	44	36	39	42	
Authentic	49	53	44	48	50	
Flexible	51	47	56	52	50	
Performance	56	59	53	53	60	
Ritual	44	41	47	47	40	
Sanctuary	77	73	81	76	79	
Auditorium	23	27	19	24	21	
Upbeat	62	62	62	63	61	
Low-Key	38	38	38	37	39	
Dignified	36	40	32	38	33	
Casual	64	60	68	62	67	
Quiet	65	65	65	64	68	
Loud	35	35	35	36	33	
Exciting	40	42	38	38	42	
Relaxed	60	58	62	62	58	
Consistency	48	52	44	50	46	
Variety	52	48	56	50	54	
Privacy	22	23	21	21	23	
Community	78	77	79	79	77	

	Ethnicity				Faith Practice				Faith Tribe				Churched Status		
	White	Black	Hispanic	All non-white	Practicing Christian	Non-practicing Christian	Other faith	No faith	Prodigals	Nomads	Exiles	Faithfuls	Churched	Marginally	Unchurched
	68%	66%	63%	68%	76%	65%	77%	57%	59%	68%	69%	76%	78%	52%	65%
	32	34	37	32	24	35	23	43	41	32	31	24	22	48	35
	60	52	60	60	43	62	54	78	71	57	43	61	48	75	63
	41	48	40	40	57	38	46	22	29	43	57	39	52	25	37
	46	49	55	55	58	47	54	37	39	39	60	55	61	40	44
	54	51	45	45	42	53	46	63	61	61	40	45	39	60	56
	56	57	58	55	59	57	50	59	57	57	60	50	56	63	55
	44	43	42	45	41	43	50	42	43	43	40	50	44	37	45
	78	80	74	76	81	82	71	65	64	83	85	77	77	87	76
	22	20	26	24	20	18	29	35	36	17	15	23	23	13	25
	61	74	69	65	72	67	56	47	61	60	77	70	68	73	57
	40	26	32	35	28	34	44	53	39	40	23	30	32	27	43
	34	33	42	39	40	31	49	31	31	31	48	34	44	30	33
	66	67	58	61	61	69	51	69	69	69	52	66	56	70	67
	64	52	71	66	57	63	79	74	70	66	57	65	67	58	67
	36	48	29	35	43	37	22	26	30	34	43	35	33	42	33
	37	59	46	46	55	41	21	33	31	33	61	41	47	46	34
	64	41	54	54	45	59	79	67	69	67	39	59	53	54	66
	48	51	48	50	58	46	48	41	32	52	55	49	61	39	44
	52	49	52	50	42	54	52	59	68	48	45	51	40	61	56
	19	11	29	24	11	18	24	38	28	19	11	10	15	12	28
	81	89	71	76	89	82	76	62	72	81	89	90	86	88	72

	Total	Gender		Age	
Table 4 | Visual Poll Part 2 Select the picture that is most appealing to you overall.		Male	Female	< 25	25 - 29
Altars					
No symbols	19%	22%	16%	15%	25%
Simple Protestant	33	30	36	34	31
Stained glass	37	38	36	38	35
White altar	11	10	12	13	9
Nature					
Paper cutouts	9	8	10	9	9
Zen planters	15	14	15	16	12
Autumn mural	15	18	11	13	16
St. Francis garden	62	60	64	61	63
Sanctuary					
Megachurch	18	20	16	18	18
Community theater	44	41	47	46	41
Chapel	20	17	23	18	23
Multipurpose room	18	22	15	19	17
Windows					
Clear and bright	35	34	36	31	40
Lilies	9	9	9	8	10
Modern geometric	22	21	22	24	19
Traditional	35	36	34	37	32

	Ethnicity				Faith Practice				Faith Tribe				Churched Status		
	White	Black	Hispanic	All non-white	Practicing Christian	Non-practicing Christian	Other faith	No faith	Prodigals	Nomads	Exiles	Faithfuls	Churched	Marginally	Unchurched
	21%	12%	19%	16%	9%	11%	51%	29%	29%	13%	12%	4%	17%	18%	21%
	38	43	14	26	40	36	25	23	28	33	34	46	37	32	31
	34	25	54	40	36	41	22	40	35	42	41	37	34	41	38
	7	21	14	17	14	13	2	8	8	11	14	13	13	8	11
	8	9	11	10	18	8	9	4	5	9	16	15	14	5	8
	14	9	17	14	5	16	14	22	19	17	10	6	6	25	17
	11	30	19	20	14	13	33	5	8	12	14	13	21	20	9
	67	52	53	56	64	62	44	69	68	63	60	66	59	51	67
	15	18	20	21	17	16	24	20	17	10	11	27	22	15	17
	42	49	48	48	42	49	34	38	41	53	51	37	39	63	42
	22	18	14	17	20	15	32	21	25	16	18	19	20	7	23
	21	15	18	15	21	19	11	20	18	21	21	17	19	16	19
	36	41	29	34	38	26	61	38	44	24	33	35	40	31	33
	11	2	4	5	6	10	6	9	7	10	6	4	6	4	11
	20	27	22	24	23	28	12	13	16	27	30	24	23	28	21
	32	29	44	38	33	36	21	39	34	39	31	38	32	37	35

	Total	Gender		Age	
Table 5 | Building Appearance How important is it to you that a building looks like a church?		Male	Female	< 25	25 - 29
Very important	16%	16%	16%	16%	16%
Somewhat important	31	31	31	30	33
Not too important	29	31	28	32	26
Not at all important	24	23	24	22	26

	Total	Gender		Age	
Table 6 | First Visit Recognition When you visit a new church, which of the following describes how you prefer to be recognized?		Male	Female	< 25	25 - 29
No recognition at all	36%	41%	32%	38%	34%
Someone notices me and introduces themselves	24	27	21	22	26
Several people notice me and introduce themselves	16	9	22	15	17
People introduce themselves, and also introduce me to others	19	18	21	19	19
The pastor or worship leader recognizes visitors by name during the service	5	6	5	6	5

	Total	Gender		Age	
Table 7 | Second Visit Recognition On your second visit to a new church, how important is it to you that someone remembers you and recognizes you?		Male	Female	< 25	25 - 29
Extremely important	11%	10%	11%	13%	8%
Somewhat important	32	29	35	28	38
Not too important	35	38	32	37	32
Not at all important	22	22	22	22	22

	Ethnicity				Faith Practice				Faith Tribe				Churched Status		
	White	Black	Hispanic	All non-white	Practicing Christian	Non-practicing Christian	Other faith	No faith	Prodigals	Nomads	Exiles	Faithfuls	Churched	Marginally	Unchurched
	10%	15%	31%	24%	27%	15%	15%	7%	4%	17%	18%	33%	27%	8%	11%
	33	36	26	30	32	40	28	13	20	39	38	33	32	50	27
	33	26	23	25	26	33	22	28	27	32	32	20	25	31	36
	24	23	21	22	16	12	35	53	48	12	12	14	16	9	31

	Ethnicity				Faith Practice				Faith Tribe				Churched Status		
	White	Black	Hispanic	All non-white	Practicing Christian	Non-practicing Christian	Other faith	No faith	Prodigals	Nomads	Exiles	Faithfuls	Churched	Marginally	Unchurched
	35%	37%	37%	38%	21%	35%	34%	55%	37%	37%	22%	22%	20%	25%	47%
	27	15	25	20	22	30	16	17	22	30	25	25	22	48	20
	17	17	11	14	24	14	13	12	15	12	18	25	21	14	13
	18	25	17	21	26	17	31	12	22	15	29	21	30	12	15
	4	7	10	7	8	5	6	5	4	6	6	6	7	2	5

	Ethnicity				Faith Practice				Faith Tribe				Churched Status		
	White	Black	Hispanic	All non-white	Practicing Christian	Non-practicing Christian	Other faith	No faith	Prodigals	Nomads	Exiles	Faithfuls	Churched	Marginally	Unchurched
	9%	10%	19%	13%	25%	7%	14%	3%	8%	7%	28%	12%	22%	3%	6%
	31	42	27	34	35	31	31	30	31	30	29	43	40	35	28
	38	30	32	31	27	44	32	25	31	41	32	31	26	53	36
	23	18	23	22	14	18	24	42	30	22	11	14	13	10	31

	Total	Gender		Age	
Table 8 | Getting Information Would you prefer to learn about the programs or activities offered through the church by ...?		Male	Female	< 25	25 - 29
Searching for that information on your own	43%	45%	42%	42%	44%
Having someone from the church tell you about the different programs	57	55	58	58	56

	Total	Gender		Age	
Table 9 | What I Want to Be Called When you visit a new church, which of the following terms best describes how you would like to be referred to?		Male	Female	< 25	25 - 29
A visitor	26%	31%	22%	26%	27%
A guest	40	34	45	40	39
Family	14	15	13	14	14
A friend	20	21	20	21	20

	Total	Gender		Age	
Table 10 | What I *Don't* Want to Be Called When you visit a church, which one of the following do you least prefer to be referred to as?		Male	Female	< 25	25 - 29
A visitor	36%	35%	37%	39%	32%
A guest	21	24	18	22	21
Family	34	32	35	32	36
A friend	10	10	10	8	12

Table 1

	Ethnicity				Faith Practice				Faith Tribe				Churched Status		
	White	Black	Hispanic	All non-white	Practicing Christian	Non-practicing Christian	Other faith	No faith	Prodigals	Nomads	Exiles	Faithfuls	Churched	Marginally	Unchurched
	49%	20%	40%	34%	28%	43%	44%	61%	46%	48%	33%	36%	30%	47%	50%
	51	80	61	66	72	57	57	39	54	52	67	64	70	53	50

Table 2

	Ethnicity				Faith Practice				Faith Tribe				Churched Status		
	White	Black	Hispanic	All non-white	Practicing Christian	Non-practicing Christian	Other faith	No faith	Prodigals	Nomads	Exiles	Faithfuls	Churched	Marginally	Unchurched
	28%	26%	18%	23%	24%	20%	36%	37%	32%	20%	22%	27%	26%	26%	27%
	41	48	32	38	43	43	30	37	35	44	46	38	42	42	38
	11	15	22	18	19	14	14	5	10	10	15	19	20	10	11
	20	11	28	22	14	23	20	21	23	26	16	16	13	22	24

Table 3

	Ethnicity				Faith Practice				Faith Tribe				Churched Status		
	White	Black	Hispanic	All non-white	Practicing Christian	Non-practicing Christian	Other faith	No faith	Prodigals	Nomads	Exiles	Faithfuls	Churched	Marginally	Unchurched
	33%	43%	43%	39%	40%	44%	28%	20%	20%	46%	44%	37%	39%	48%	31%
	19	28	21	24	24	21	28	10	18	19	19	32	27	19	18
	39	24	24	26	24	28	42	55	51	26	21	28	25	26	40
	9	5	13	11	12	7	3	15	11	8	17	4	10	7	10

	Total	Gender		Age	
Table 11 | Preferred Follow Up After your first visit to a new church, how comfortable would you be with each type of follow up?		Male	Female	< 25	25 - 29
An email acknowledging your visit					
Very comfortable	30%	27%	33%	32%	28%
Somewhat comfortable	33	31	35	30	36
Not too comfortable	17	17	16	19	14
Not at all comfortable	21	25	16	20	21
A note in the mail					
Very comfortable	34	29	38	36	31
Somewhat comfortable	36	34	37	34	39
Not too comfortable	13	17	9	14	12
Not at all comfortable	17	19	15	16	19
A care package (like cookies or small gifts)					
Very comfortable	28	25	31	29	26
Somewhat comfortable	32	34	31	31	34
Not too comfortable	18	18	18	19	17
Not at all comfortable	22	24	20	21	23
A gift card (as a "thanks for visiting")					
Very comfortable	31	28	35	33	28
Somewhat comfortable	35	36	34	35	36
Not too comfortable	13	14	12	14	12
Not at all comfortable	21	22	19	18	24
A phone call from someone at the church					
Very comfortable	15	14	16	15	15
Somewhat comfortable	27	30	24	30	24
Not too comfortable	29	26	32	25	34
Not at all comfortable	28	30	27	30	27

	Ethnicity				Faith Practice				Faith Tribe				Churched Status		
	White	Black	Hispanic	All non-white	Practicing Christian	Non-practicing Christian	Other faith	No faith	Prodigals	Nomads	Exiles	Faithfuls	Churched	Marginally	Unchurched
	28%	43%	31%	34%	50%	31%	25%	14%	22%	32%	56%	32%	41%	25%	25%
	36	30	28	28	30	37	22	28	33	31	21	51	36	50	27
	20	7	14	13	12	16	24	19	14	18	10	11	13	15	19
	17	20	28	25	9	16	29	39	31	19	13	6	11	10	29
	33	46	32	35	51	36	28	16	27	39	57	33	42	41	27
	37	39	30	34	29	43	27	32	32	39	25	42	35	41	35
	14	4	16	12	10	11	24	15	13	11	7	13	13	8	15
	16	11	22	19	10	10	21	37	27	11	11	12	10	10	23
	27	43	28	30	39	27	31	18	28	27	45	23	32	37	24
	32	29	35	34	26	40	23	23	22	35	24	43	33	34	31
	22	13	11	13	19	18	17	20	21	18	18	16	17	17	19
	20	15	26	24	16	15	29	39	29	20	14	18	17	13	26
	28	44	35	36	46	33	30	16	24	37	48	36	41	33	26
	37	41	32	33	29	41	26	35	37	34	28	35	32	45	35
	15	4	8	10	8	12	20	16	15	12	6	9	9	8	16
	20	11	26	22	17	15	26	33	24	17	18	19	18	15	23
	13	31	14	19	29	12	22	7	10	12	30	12	25	16	10
	27	29	30	29	37	32	22	7	13	30	34	48	39	27	21
	33	19	27	23	23	32	31	30	40	29	17	30	24	39	29
	27	21	29	30	11	25	25	56	36	28	19	10	13	19	40

	Total	Gender		Age	
Table 11 | Cont.		Male	Female	< 25	25 - 29
A visit at home from someone at the church					
Very comfortable	8%	7%	9%	7%	9%
Somewhat comfortable	18	20	16	19	16
Not too comfortable	28	26	30	26	30
Not at all comfortable	46	47	45	48	45

	Total	Gender		Age	
Table 12 | Sharing Information When you visit a new church for the first time, which of the following pieces of information are you comfortable giving to the church?		Male	Female	< 25	25 - 29
Your first name	82%	78%	86%	82%	83%
Your last name	53	54	52	55	50
Your home address	19	17	22	20	18
Your personal email address	33	29	38	35	32
Your home phone number	16	14	18	18	13
Your personal cell phone number	13	12	14	14	11
Social media addresses (Facebook, Twitter, etc.)	6	6	6	6	5
None of these	15	18	12	16	13

* Indicates less than one half of one percent

	Ethnicity				Faith Practice				Faith Tribe				Churched Status		
	White	Black	Hispanic	All non-white	Practicing Christian	Non-practicing Christian	Other faith	No faith	Prodigals	Nomads	Exiles	Faithfuls	Churched	Marginally	Unchurched
	5%	17%	12%	12%	19%	5%	16%	*	3%	3%	16%	12%	17%	3%	4%
	18	15	22	19	25	18	21	6	11	14	26	33	29	25	10
	29	32	22	26	30	34	23	17	23	34	28	26	28	32	27
	48	35	44	43	27	44	41	77	63	49	30	30	26	40	59

	Ethnicity				Faith Practice				Faith Tribe				Churched Status		
	White	Black	Hispanic	All non-white	Practicing Christian	Non-practicing Christian	Other faith	No faith	Prodigals	Nomads	Exiles	Faithfuls	Churched	Marginally	Unchurched
	87%	81%	76%	77%	91%	85%	82%	70%	79%	90%	90%	85%	90%	92%	76%
	56	60	46	49	67	57	49	30	47	62	68	58	66	63	44
	22	15	17	15	29	22	17	5	13	25	23	28	27	24	15
	36	33	33	31	47	34	36	21	36	34	49	38	40	48	27
	17	22	13	15	26	16	18	4	14	22	18	23	21	20	12
	14	12	13	11	21	11	11	8	8	16	17	15	17	23	8
	6	8	7	6	13	5	3	1	4	4	14	8	10	7	3
	12	16	15	17	2	12	18	29	19	9	5	4	2	7	23

METHODOLOGY

FIELD GROUPS (QUALITATIVE)

The focus groups were conducted on August 26 and 27, 2013, in Atlanta, Georgia, and Chicago, Illinois. In each city, 10 adults ages 18 to 29 were recruited by a local research recruiting firm. They were told that the groups were about religion and architecture, but that no background in either was required. Participants were screened from a variety of religious backgrounds, including practicing Christians, non-practicing Christians and non-Christians, and came from a range of racial and ethnic backgrounds, including black, white, Hispanic and Arab. Each group had at least three male participants.

On August 26, the Atlanta group toured Buckhead Church, Lutheran Church of the Redeemer, Centennial Park and a local Starbucks. On August 27, the Chicago group toured Willow Creek Community Church (Barrington), St. James Episcopal Cathedral, Millennium Park and Intelligentsia Coffee. At each location the participants were asked how they perceived each space, and how they would use it. They were also asked general questions about religious facilities and their perceptions of Christian churches. Each group lasted approximately six hours. All participants were compensated for their time.

NATIONAL STUDIES (QUANTITATIVE)

Throughout this Barna Report are statistics and research findings that are not directly footnoted, because these data and data-based statements are derived from original research designed and conducted by Barna Group. The primary basis of this report is the Barna/CKN Millennials and Architecture poll, which included 843 online surveys conducted among adult residents of the United States ages 18 to 29, from October 10 through October 15, 2013. The margin of error for a sample of this size is plus or minus 5.2 percentage points, at the 95% confidence level.

In addition to the CKN national survey, data from the Barna FRAMES project was also used in the creation of this report. The FRAMES project included four separate nationwide studies conducted between May and August 2013. These public opinion studies were conducted using a mix of telephone (including cell phones) and online interviewing among 4,495 U.S. adults. The maximum sampling error for any of the four studies is plus or minus 3.1 percentage points at the 95% confidence level.

The surveys administered online for these studies used a research panel called KnowledgePanel® based on probability sampling that covers both the online and offline populations in the U.S. The panel members are randomly recruited by telephone and by self-administered mail and web surveys. Households are provided with access to the Internet and hardware if needed. Unlike other Internet surveys that cover only individuals with Internet access who volunteer for research, this process uses a dual sampling frame that includes both listed and unlisted phone numbers, telephone and non-telephone households and cell-phone-only households. The panel is not limited to current Web users or computer owners. All potential panelists are randomly selected to join the KnowledgePanel; unselected volunteers are not able to join.

Email reminders were sent out to non-responders on day three of the fielding period. In every survey there are a variety of ways in which the accuracy of the data may be affected. The response rate is one such potential cause of error in measurement; the lower the response, the less representative the respondents surveyed may be of the population from which they were drawn, thereby reducing the accuracy of the results. Other sources of error include question-design bias, question-order bias, sampling error and respondent deception. Many of these types of errors cannot be accurately estimated. However, having a high cooperation rate does enhance the reliability of the information procured.

Minimal statistical weighting was used to calibrate the sample to known population percentages in relation to demographic variables.

Making Space for Millennials also includes survey results from original Barna Group research conducted for Brad Lomenick's book *The Catalyst Leader* (Thomas Nelson, 2013). Used by permission.

In its 30-year history, Barna Group has conducted more than one million interviews over the course of hundreds of studies, and has become a go-to source for insights about faith and culture, leadership and vocation, and generations. Currently led by David Kinnaman, Barna Group's vision is to provide people with credible knowledge and clear thinking, enabling them to navigate a complex and changing culture. The company was started by George and Nancy Barna in 1984.

Barna Group has worked with thousands of businesses, nonprofit organizations and churches across the country, including many Protestant denominations and Catholic parishes. Some of its clients include the American Bible Society, CARE, Compassion International, Dreamworks, Easter Seals, Habitat for Humanity, NBC-Universal, Paramount Pictures, The Salvation Army, Walden Media, the ONE Campaign, SONY, Thrivent, USAID and World Vision.

The firm's studies are frequently cited in sermons and talks, and its public opinion research is often quoted in major media outlets such as CNN, *USA Today*, *The Wall Street Journal*, Fox News, *Chicago Tribune*, *Huffington Post*, the *New York Times*, *Dallas Morning News* and the *Los Angeles Times*.

Learn more about Barna Group at www.barna.org.

The Cornerstone Knowledge Network (CKN) is a select group of innovative companies that collaborates to develop exclusive insights into the alignment of:

- Culture

- Leadership

- Ministry

- Facilities

CKN's mission is to discover and disseminate meaningful knowledge that radically improves how church facilities impact ministry.

The two founding companies, Aspen Group and Cogun, offer valuable information as well as proven consulting services to ministry teams. They are committed to helping these teams develop an empowering missional ministry that has a transforming impact on their community.

CKN looks forward to welcoming you to an Alignment Conference. This acclaimed church building seminar is a clearinghouse of the latest information you need to assure your construction project is on a firm foundation.

Visit CKN at www.theckn.com.